Getting a grip on TIME

Take control…
achieve your
goals… and have
the time of your life!

Robyn Pearce

Best wishes
Robyn Pearce

REED

Published by Reed Books, an imprint of Reed Publishing (NZ) Ltd,
39 Rawene Road, Birkenhead, Auckland 10. Associated companies, branches and
representatives throughout the world.

ISBN 0 7900 0470 4

First published 1996
Reprinted 1998

Cartoons by Ron Hoares
Front cover designed by Chris Lipscombe
Text designed by Clair Stutton

Printed in New Zealand

Contents

To my dear husband, Mike —

*who has uncomplainingly supported me through the
weird and unsociable behaviour of the writer's habit;*

*who has never complained when the Muse called
me in the middle of the night, even when he's
had cold feet on his back;*

*who has not minded a small travelling companion —
my trusty laptop —
when we went on holiday to lovely places.*

Thank you.

Acknowledgements

To the wonderful people who have attended my speeches and courses, thank you for sharing your struggles, triumphs, and knowledge. This book would never have been born without you.

Also to Garry Halliday, Terry and Kingsley Kalaf, and Chris Disspain, authors of the *Fuller LiFE MAP* (1995), who have allowed me to use excerpts from the Fuller LiFE MAP methodology in the first part of the book. Fuller LiFE MAPs are a dynamic and accelerated way of identifying your goals. Thank you, team.

And thank you to friends around New Zealand who made it possible for me to have quiet space for writing. Being in a wee crib on the Otago Peninsula in March 1995 is a memory I treasure. Thank you Neill, Helen, Helena, Ron and Bridgit. Heather, if you hadn't been keeping the office running so efficiently I could never have taken the time to go to those quiet places. You made this book possible and I thank you, with love.

Preface

There's a better way

If you struggle with getting a grip on your time, run frantically round in circles, and know that if only the day were a bit longer you'd be able to catch up, welcome.

If the people with tidy desks really brass you off, the punctual ones always look smug as you slide red-faced into the room, and you hate the look on your boss's face when you have to ask for an extension of time, take heart.

If you've ever been shut out of a meeting because you were too late, missed the chance of important business because you made a bad impression with your lateness, and forgotten a most urgent deadline because the relevant information was buried under a mountain of paper, hope is round the corner.

If your family seem to be constantly commenting on your work load, your friends say, 'We never see you these days', and life seems to be rapidly passing you by, take time to read.

If, with laughter and with anguish, you have said, 'I just want a life', this book is for you.

Truly, life is at hand — in your hands. I've been through all the charming experiences above, worked with many others who have specialised in the same delightful habits, and the good news is: *there is a better way.*

PART

1

Common-sense personal
management for all of
your life, not just the
work bits

Chapter 1

Finding a road map for effective and successful living

We seem to be living in a whole new world. People are learning to act and react in different ways, there are new ways of doing business, and constantly we hear of new approaches to old problems, including the way we use our lives and our time.

But I believe that we're just rediscovering the best of the old ways — the people-based, principle-based behaviours that have always been the cornerstone of effective societies.

Today's top speakers, motivators and educators in business management, for example, talk about the principle of going the extra mile, of caring about the people you deal with, of doing more than expected, of surprising with dazzlingly superb service. And yet many people have lived their lives by this basic philosophy. It is not new, but it is good to hear it being advocated again, both in the business world as well as for everyday life.

Similarly the teaching on customer service excellence, and relationship or integrity selling, is based on the age-old principles of honour, trust and integrity. We've gone through a time of the 'fast buck', the 'me first, you fight your own battles' thinking, the era of the sleazy salesperson whom no-one trusts and whose manipulative techniques push people into buying things they don't really want. No wonder salespeople gained such a bad name. The 'modern' emphasis is on discovering the client's needs and being of service.

It is now also recognised that we take more pride in our work and work better if we can do complete tasks and work in well-functioning teams, as our forebears did in pre-industrial times. Piece work, assembly lines, punching time clocks, working as the union dictates, and giving unquestioning obedience to the company line are workplace practices that have come under close scrutiny in recent years. Today, the emphasis is on developing high-performing teams, encouraging participative management, and improving communication.

Despite these positive changes, I often hear people who attend my courses ask, 'Why has the pace of life got so hectic?' They pine for a simpler life, for better ways of doing things, for a sense of balance and harmony in their lives. There is an increasing hunger for quality personal time, for spiritual truth instead of institution-alised dogma, for good health, and for a balanced lifestyle. It is possible.

HOW TO USE THIS BOOK

There is, indeed, nothing new under the sun, but there are new insights to be gained from rediscovering the old messages. This book will take you on that old/new journey. It is my journey and the journey of others; a journey to rediscover harmony, balance, and effective living. It is also a journey of common sense and practical application.

In the mid-eighties I was a solo mother, struggling to survive. My commercial experience was nil. Eventually I ended up in a major city. With my limited business skills and knowledge it was a challenge, but an exciting one — a challenge that I grasped with both hands. It didn't take me very long to realise that, although I was a very hard worker, one of my weaknesses and limiting habits was the way I used my time. Although I got good results it was often at the expense of my health and my personal time. There had to be a better way. When, as a burnt-out real estate agent I heard my first talk on time management, it was like mana from heaven. There were simple steps I could take, new practical skills I could learn, that would help me work smarter, not harder.

This book is the road map of knowledge I've gained from extensive study on how to be effective, successful, and enjoy great quality of life. It is also full of many practical tips I wish I'd known years ago.

Its purpose is to help you achieve your goals, whatever they are — not to imitate what other people do. Treat the information offered you as a smorgasbord — help yourself to what works for you. Most importantly, relax with it — the aim is to enhance your life, not constrain it.

About half the world's population operates from the right-brain, creative orientation; the other, more logical souls are clear-thinking, sequential, list-making left-brainers. Trying to make the creative free spirits follow exactly the methods of the rest of the world is to fight a losing battle. It reminds me of the saying, 'It's no use trying to teach a pig to sing. It annoys the pig, and frustrates the heck out of you.'

So, my creative friends, use what works, adapt what you need, have fun with the information, get your coloured pens and paper out, be zany, and take control. However, don't use your right-brain orientation as an excuse to be disorganised and non-achieving. Creative people can be very organised, too. If you don't believe me, have a look at Ann McGee-Cooper and Duane Trammell's book *Time Management for Unmanageable People* (1994).

While I love order and logic, I also love fun, spontaneity, and flexibility. In this book, therefore, you'll get a straightforward, common-sense approach to personal management, with no apologies for a touch of humour. And you'll find information here of value to you, no matter how seemingly disorganised you are at present.

WHAT IS THIS THING CALLED TIME MANAGEMENT?

KEY POINT No. 1: This moment of time is a non-renewable resource. It will never come again.

We can't really *manage* time. Once we've used this minute, this 30 minutes, it's gone. It's irreplaceable. We can't save it or store it — we can only spend it.

In fact, time management is a misnomer. It is *life management* above all else. And the tricky thing about life is, according to Garry Halliday, joint creator of the Fuller LiFE MAP, that it is 'multiple events, occurring simultaneously, moving in many directions'.

So, how do we control these seemingly uncontrollable 'multiple events'? What we *can* do is manage ourselves. In fact, if we fail to do so, then the events will control us. And when this happens we experience tension, stress, depression and unhappiness.

FOCUS

What makes us good at handling time? How can we become more effective in the various areas of our lives? What makes a person a 'success'? I believe that *focus* is the key.

Be aware that there is a very fine line between failing and succeeding. People who fail often work as hard as those who succeed. The major difference is that successful people are more productive. The failures wheel-spin and don't prioritise. They don't understand the magic power of focus.

> KEY POINT No. 2: There is no such thing as lack of time, only lack of focus. We can all do the things we really want to do.

WHAT CHOICES DO WE HAVE?

Often we can see all sorts of problems in the situations around us. The boss pushes us into reactive mode . . . our partner is always late . . . our children stress us to the maximum . . . there are always interruptions in our day . . . the traffic was too heavy today . . . and so we could go on.

Somewhere we have to stop and say: 'I'm part of this situation, so I am also part of the solution. How can I make a difference?'

At first we tend to think we don't have choices. We feel pushed and pulled by the twists of fate. Not so: we can choose at every step of the way. There are always things we can do — sometimes only small things — that will, in the long term, make a significant difference to our lives. Quite small shifts in understanding, or attitude, and therefore in action, can give us huge long-term benefits. Getting a handle on time usage is not about waving a magic wand — it's about many small, unseen, unsung steps that lead you to the destination of your choosing.

Did you realise that as soon as you start responding in a slightly different way to any set of circumstances, you alter their effects? For instance, you can alter the effect of the traffic by leaving twenty minutes earlier, and having breakfast in town. Then you won't be stressed by the rush hour. You've got children to organise? Do their lunches the night before, and make sure all their clothes are ready for the morning. Get them up ten minutes earlier.

Remember, there's no such thing as lack of time, only lack of focus. We can all do the things we really want to do by focusing on what really matters.

> KEY POINT No. 3: There are always ways to change
> things, but if you believe you can't, you won't.

EFFICIENCY VERSUS EFFECTIVENESS

It is possible to be efficient, and yet not be effective. An effective person achieves the right results with minimum fuss. They are clear about their over-riding purpose and day-to-day objectives, and do not waste time on activities which do not support that purpose.

However, many people consider themselves very efficient, but they've forgotten to take a compass bearing on where they're heading. They are so busy doing things right that they forget to notice whether they are doing the right things!

We can patch up our old habits by applying some new time management practices, but if we don't understand *why* we're doing what we're doing, the chance of sustaining those practices is pretty slim once the first flush of enthusiasm passes or when a crisis hits. Those who have not taken this reality check often wonder why long-term peace of mind and personal satisfaction don't follow their improved efficiency. They still feel stressed out, even though they know they're wasting less time on unproductive habits. They regularly feel as though the tail is wagging the dog, that they never seem to catch up, no matter how efficient they are. Familiar? Such people are almost always focusing on being efficient and not taking time to consider how they can be most effective.

The foundation of good time management is finding out what matters deeply to you — what it is you really want to achieve in life.

KEY POINT No. 4: There's no point in learning to be efficient if we're efficiently doing the wrong things.

ANYONE YOU KNOW? PITFALLS TO AVOID!

Some people *know* they have a challenge with time management. Others think they're good at it, but are they? Do you know anyone who has any of the following traits?

Uptight Arthur

Arthur is absolutely fanatical about *always* being on time. If others keep him waiting even a minute he starts showing signs that an anxiety attack is coming on! Keep him waiting five minutes and his stress levels are soaring! He thinks he's good at time management, and so he is on the organisational level, but he's very uncomfortable to be around, can't relax and be flexible, and isn't very good at going with the flow, or re-prioritising when something needs urgent attention or crises come up (which happens in everyone's life). Time controls him, not the other way around.

Frenetic Frances

Here we have the person who is *always* busy — but those around her are never exactly sure what it is that keeps her on her perpetual-motion treadmill. Frenetic Frances isn't exactly sure either. She doesn't know how to take time out to recharge, isn't good at putting first things first, seldom stops to reflect on where this endless round of activity is taking her. She certainly achieves quite a bit — but is she achieving what matters? She is always *so busy* being busy!

Lewis the List-maker
Lewis loves lists. He writes down everything. He never forgets things, because it's all been recorded, but he's so busy planning and getting organised that effective action often doesn't follow. He's a great fellow, loves detail, but is a bad initiator. Someone else has to tell him what to do, or nothing of any consequence happens.

Sloppy Samantha
Here we have someone who would traditionally be recognised as bad at time management. She's so relaxed, able to go with the flow, and easily distracted that she drives any

organised person nuts. She is hardly ever on time, forgets things because writing anything down is *such* a drag, and achieves half of what she should because she's always good for a chat. Don't rely on Samantha!

In truth, most of us exhibit elements of all these behaviour styles from time to time. The trick is to recognise what you're doing, and fix it!

A WARNING BEFORE WE START — THE PLACE OF DISCIPLINE

If you're reading this book for a quick fix, you're out of luck, and I can't help you ! Self-discipline over a period of time, and a determination to improve, are key elements in better time management.

Be aware, however, that we can only change one thing at a time. Don't try to improve everything simultaneously — you'll blow yourself away. Choose one area of your life and work on that for 21 days — then the change will have become a habit. Then work on another area.

Don't be too hard on yourself when you slip

up — as you will. Praise yourself for what you've achieved and get back to the new habits. How long did you take to learn the old ones? You've practised them for a lifetime, haven't you? Don't be unrealistic about how long new habits will take to learn, but don't use that as an excuse not to get started! Winners know they won't reform overnight. They're prepared to take the slow road of small, regular improvements in order to get into more productive habits.

KEY POINT No. 5: I will do today what others won't, so I can have tomorrow what others can't.

Chapter 2

Let's get started

FINDING THE SOLID GROUND FOR OUR LADDER OF LIFE

If we don't base our lives, and therefore our actions, on the solid foundation of certain timeless and unchangeable laws of life, we could be learning many wonderful tips on efficiency, but totally missing the point about effectiveness. Who wants to be a Frenetic Frances, forever running around in circles? In this chapter we are going to briefly look at some of these fundamental principles for effective living.

Let's get started by thinking of life as a ladder. Some people scramble up through the years without ever checking to see if their ladder is on solid ground or up against the right wall. We need to make sure that what we thought we were aiming for at the beginning is what we're going to find at the top. And in terms of how we use our time, the most vital thing is to be spending it on what really matters. So how do we decide? To answer that important question we are going to climb up the rungs of our Ladder of Life, checking each rung as we go.

But first we have to make sure we've got our ladder on the firm base that those principles provide — otherwise we'll be in for a shaky time of it. Look around you at the people you admire. In probably every case they will seem to have a clear focus — they will know where they're going in life. It doesn't matter whether they are 'important' in the business world. They will be people of integrity and influence. They will live their lives based on firm foundations. They will be principled people.

Stephen Covey's *7 Habits of Highly Effective People* (1990) is just one book which has made a big impact on the thinking in this area. It highlights the importance of looking more closely at the principles that, through time, effective societies, communities, businesses, families and individuals have recognised and followed.

PRINCIPLES FOR EFFECTIVE LIVING

So what are these principles? Other writers, such as Covey, cover the subject in depth — the purpose of discussing them in this book is only as a brief introduction to the latest time management knowledge.

I think that some of the saddest people around are those who haven't taken the time to learn that true personal power comes from within, from basing their lives on certain fundamental principles. It doesn't come from status, expensive toys, the right address, control of other people, and how many influential names they can drop into conversation. It comes from the heart, the soul, and connecting with truth.

Let's look at some specific illustrations. The people who say: 'Me first, you fend for yourself' operate from a selfish perspective, ignoring the laws of the universe, nature, God, a Higher Power, or whoever or whatever we choose to acknowledge. Their attitude declares 'All that "do unto others as you'd have them do unto you" stuff is irrelevant. I'm only interested in what's in it for me.'

Others are always looking for short cuts and quick fixes, instead of being prepared to take the time to put in the necessary groundwork. They're impatient.

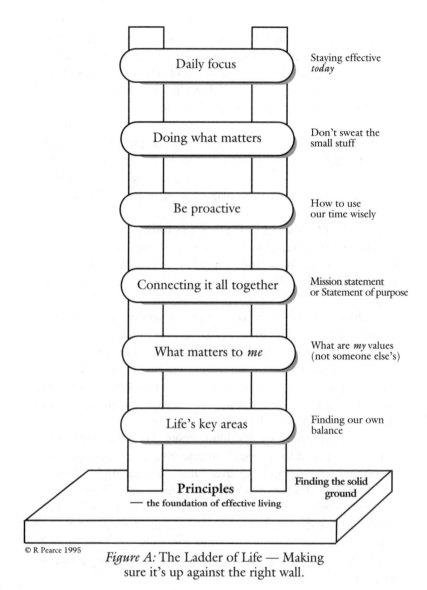

Staying effective
today

Don't sweat the
small stuff

How to use
our time wisely

Mission statement
or Statement of purpose

What are *my* values
(not someone else's)

Finding our own
balance

Finding the solid
ground

Daily focus

Doing what matters

Be proactive

Connecting it all together

What matters to *me*

Life's key areas

Principles
— the foundation of effective living

© R Pearce 1995

Figure A: The Ladder of Life — Making
sure it's up against the right wall.

We reap what we sow. Look around you. Selfish people live a small-minded, closed existence, physically and mentally blocking the free flow of love and generosity. They make judgements about others' motives based on their own. People who live with suspicion fight with fear — they see danger around every corner. Those who don't trust their fellows are always experiencing someone taking them down. The ones who fill their minds with hate and anger are unloved and unlovable. The people who fear ill-health are constantly sick — it is their only topic of conversation. Those who fear poverty are always poor — their minds are constantly occupied by their lack of wealth. Those who use quick-fix, short-term solutions get short-term results.

The irony is that the people who operate in these ways are living proof of the very principles they are ignoring. If we spend time understanding what these fundamental universal principles are, and learn to base our lives and the use of time around them, we soon start to feel a sense of power and control in our lives. And, what's more, we get much better results with much less stress.

Take the analogy of creating a garden. As any gardener who understands how to create good gardens knows, it is necessary to make thorough preparation.

My husband used not to know much about gardening. When helping me put a truckload of good topsoil on a new garden bed, he became very impatient. He liked the pretty picture at the end but hadn't appreciated how much spade-work went into achieving that result! His suggestion was: 'This is too slow. Why don't we just dig some holes where the plants are going to be placed, put the soil in so the plant isn't straight into clay, and let nature take its course?'

For a brief moment, the idea tempted me! I ask, do you enjoy shovelling metres of topsoil? However, my more advanced knowledge of horticulture wouldn't let either of us off the hook that easily. I explained about the basic principles of gardening. If we hadn't observed them, our time would have been wasted. When the roots reached the outer perimeter of their rich soil, most of them would have curled up their toes and died. Others would have been waterlogged because the topsoil would be so much more free-draining than the surrounding clay. My husband may not have enjoyed shovelling soil, but no amount of wishing was going to change the fact that proper preparation was necessary if we were going to get the long-term results we wanted. The principle here was that excellent preparation would give excellent results, while poor preparation would give poor results.

Let's think of a human relationship example. All of us at times have had a lengthy wait in a queue. Have you ever noticed how an impatient person can take away the composure of the people around them? Smiles disappear, tension is created, and the person goes away muttering about bad service. On the other hand, the calm, serene person who smiles sends a positive message to others, and goes away having had a good experience. The principle here is that what we give out is what we get back.

Peace of mind comes through connecting with the right principles.

Exercise 1

Here's a list of some principles of effective living, and a chance for you to add more. Write a sentence, or a few words, about what each word means to you, and how much importance it has for you.

For example:

Trust   To be able to trust and be trusted by the people I associate with is very important to me.

Good attitude A positive, forward-looking approach to life. A willingness to consider the viewpoint of others.

What other principles can you think of? Write a few words, or a sentence about them also.

Modern time management starts from a solid base of such principles, and as we go on the reason for this will become clearer.

Now we've got our ladder securely on solid ground, let's take the first step up.

Trust	Patience	Good attitude
Integrity	Industry	Dignity
Humility	Simplicity	Service
Fidelity	Modesty	Quality
Temperance	Diligence	The 'Golden Rule'
Courage	Fairness	Respect
Justice	Honesty	Love

KEY POINT No. 6: If we have a clear picture of what matters to us, our actions today will put flesh on our dreams and we won't drift aimlessly through life.

Chapter 3

Finding our balance and discovering our values

THE FIRST RUNG — LIFE'S KEY AREAS

Let's take a relaxed and simple look at what our life consists of.

In my courses we look at four key areas: Self and Wellbeing, Business and Career, Home and Family, Community and Humanity. Notice that Self and Wellbeing is first on this list — quite deliberately, I assure you. It's vital to include ourselves, not from a selfish, 'me first' perspective, but because if we forget to look after ourselves we eventually end up burning out, with nothing left to offer our family, our business associates, or anyone else. Even a small amount of focus on self helps keep a healthy balance and enables us to be more effective people.

The first rung of the ladder represents these key areas.

Exercise 2

This is a 'whole-of-life' look at your roles in life — the hats you wear. First, look at the example in Figure B; then take a large sheet of paper and draw Figure C on it, large enough for you to write on. You're now going to map out the key components of your life, as it is at present. Use coloured pens. Have fun. Life is too important to be deadly serious about!

Bear in mind that your work may consist of several distinct types of activity. For example, you may have a customer service role, a sales role, and a management function. If so, record them separately. Don't just write 'work' on your chart.

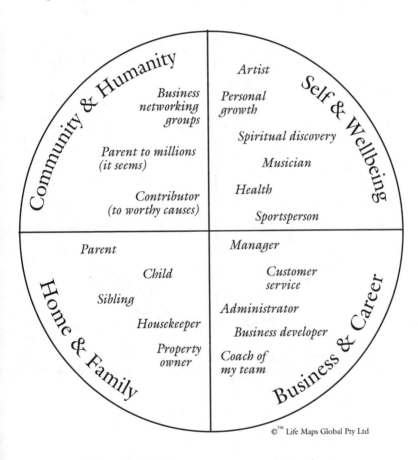

Figure B: Life's key areas — example quadrant.

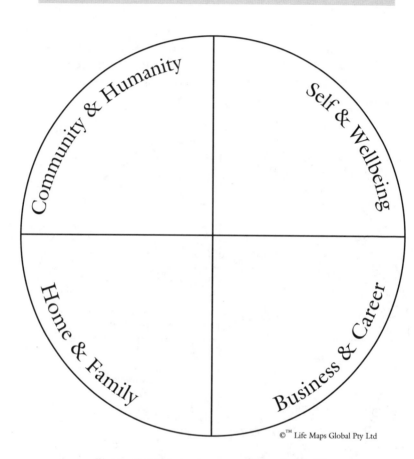

Figure C: Life's key areas — My roles in life.
Record the different roles you have in the segments of your life.

THE SECOND RUNG OF THE LADDER — WHAT MATTERS TO ME?

The next step up the ladder is to look at what you as an individual value, what your hot buttons are, what personal standards and issues you get passionate about.

You may well ask: 'What's the difference between principles and values?'

My perspective is that principles are changeless; values are personal. Principles are much bigger than any person; they are truly foundational. Values, however, vary from person to person, and what is a high value to you right now may not be as highly important to you in another few years. However, I believe that the more principle-based our values are, the more power we can tap into.

For example, money as such is neither good nor bad, but a principle of effective living is that if we invest our money in things such as property, education, and personal and professional development, with a long-term vision instead of a short-term desire for instant gratification, we will be much more likely to prosper and live a comfortable life. Although most of us basically agree with that, at various times of our lives we may put more value on, say, travel, new experiences, and living in the moment, rather than on being a good squirrel and stashing dollars in the bank, buying property, or getting educated.

Let's take health as another example. A principle would be: *The right combination of wholesome food, a positive attitude, exercise and sleep will promote good health.* However, maybe you are working extra time to complete a major project or set up a new business, which is your number one priority right now, and so you choose to do very little exercise.

It's okay to ignore principles such as these for a time, if you understand what you're doing, but it's foolish never to self-correct, because then you'll be one of those people who rush blind-ly on closing your mind to the basic laws of effective living, and then wonder why you're poor or sick a few years down the track.

TAKING TIME TO DISCOVER OUR VALUES — THE POWER OF THE PEN

Have you ever spent a quiet hour or more thinking about your values, and drawing them or writing them down? Many people will say, 'Oh, I know what's important to me. Why do I need to record it?'

Have you noticed that putting your thoughts down on paper forces clarity?

I believe that we have a channel from our brain to our fingers, which empties as we record the thoughts we hold in our mind. When the channel is empty, new original thoughts come from beyond ourselves. Ask any writer if they know the details of their work before they start. They may know the end of their story, or the outline, but no-one I know can see the material complete in every detail. In writing this book, for example, I began with a clear idea of what I wanted to say, but each time I sat down at the computer I saw ways I could express my message more clearly. As I crafted the words, the message became clearer to me. So with recording our values.

I strongly encourage you to spend time considering what really matters to you. Don't attempt it with other people around you — you must have 'alone time'. It won't be easy at first, but the feel-ing of having the power to control your life that comes out of the exercise far exceeds the pain of creating your island of time and learning to look inward.

So, what are your own personal values? What really matters to you at this stage of your life? *Remember, they must be your values, no-one else's.*

Recognise that people's values will vary, and that is okay. For instance, the people you know probably differ from you in their views on how important money and financial success are. There's no absolute right or wrong here, though trying to impose our values on other people *is* wrong! What matters to each of us is what *our* values are.

Having a clear idea about our principles and values provides us with road markers when it comes to making decisions about how to use our time.

For instance, you may want to join a sports club and participate very regularly, because you value keeping fit. You may also want to stand for election to a local political organisation because you value contributing to your local community, and because it will give you good networking contacts for business. When you analyse the time commitments required for both activities, you may have to make a choice because you are so busy that there's only time for one. They are both worthwhile activities, but you've decided that you can't manage both.

So, which do you choose? There is no 'right' answer. Each individual has to decide for themselves, on the basis of what is the priority for them at the time. The key element is knowing clearly *what* is important. Many people try too hard to fit in everything (I've done it myself many times). The result is that nothing is done well, leaving a sense of dissatisfaction for all concerned.

And a work example? Suppose you are at work, nearly ready to leave, and the boss comes in with an urgent bit of work that she wants to discuss, right then. She could have asked your opinion any time in the last four hours, but didn't think of it. You, however, have promised your wife that you will take her out for dinner. You're trying to accrue Brownie points with your wife because you've been working so hard lately that she's feeling rather neglected.

Your boss is a thoroughly nice person, but she's rather reactive and tends to 'last-minute' both herself and her staff. She expects you to be Mr Nice Guy and put your own agendas aside in order to help her. However, if you have a clear perspective on your personal values and therefore on your priorities, it will be much easier to suggest an alternative solution, such as coming in earlier tomorrow, or discussing it on the car phone as you drive home. Being proactive and making a stand for your family values will also send a message to the boss. She will be much less likely to last-minute you next time.

> KEY POINT No. 7: A clear set of values, knowing what is important to *you*, helps you make wise decisions about using your time.

Exercise 3

We're now going to link your results from Exercise 2 with your discovery of your own personal values.

Again, first you have an example (Figure D), and then a chance to explore and record your own ideas (Figure E). There is no right or wrong — write, draw, put sentences, words, or diagrams on your chart. Listen to your inner thoughts. Relax with the exercise. Whatever you write does not commit you forever to what you may say today.

Some of the same values may apply in more than one area. That's okay. Record what matters to you, in each area.

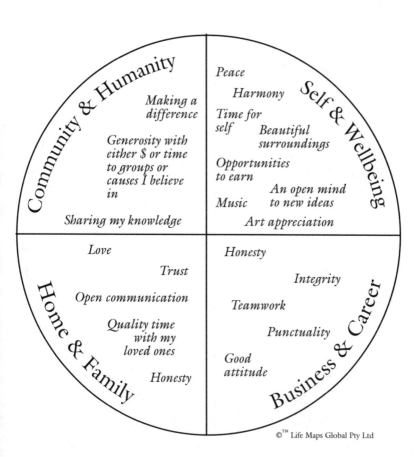

Figure D: What do I value? Example quadrant.

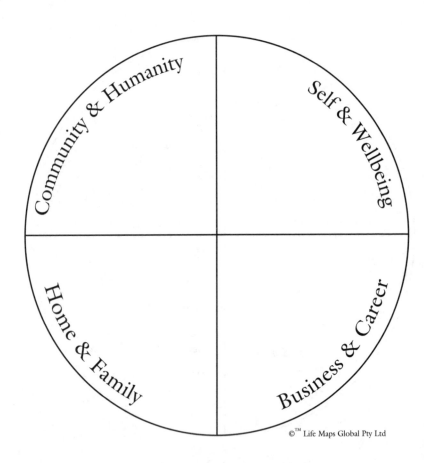

© ™ Life Maps Global Pty Ltd

Figure E: What do I value?
Record your values in each segment of your life.

As we've already mentioned, the writing down of all these thoughts is a very important part of the process. A landscaper on one of my courses had this to say:

> I remember when I started. It was very difficult at first to make myself begin to write, and it took me a long time to work out why. Finally I realised that it felt scary. It was like making a commitment, even if only to myself. And it takes self-discipline to sit and do the writing. We live in a busy world, a world of instant action and quick entertainment, and it's easier to cruise through life with a comfortable, but only general, awareness of what our most important issues are. Somehow, writing them down made them more serious. I think I'd been scared of what I might find when I looked more closely inside my head. In fact, it was a very liberating experience, once I'd started.

KEY POINT No. 8: If you know what you stand for, you are on the road to reaching your full potential.

Chapter 4

What are we here for?

THE THIRD RUNG OF THE LADDER — STATEMENT OF PURPOSE

We are now ready for the third rung, where we link together all the issues we've discussed so far. Some people call it a mission statement, others a statement of purpose. Not everybody bothers to do this step, but those who make the extra effort all comment with passion about how it gives them a sharper, clearer focus on their life.

In fact, it goes further and deeper than this. For some people having a clear sense of purpose gives them the cutting edge which enables them to achieve their chosen goals in life; for others it has actually been life-saving.

Viktor Frankl (who died in 1997, aged 92) was the famous Jewish psychiatrist who survived four concentration camps and wrote *Man's Search for Meaning* (1959). He found that no matter what the external conditions — and I doubt if any of us could think of conditions worse than those the Jews experienced in places like Auschwitz — when people had a purpose to live, a vision of something they still wanted to do, they kept on surviving against impossible odds.

Napoleon Hill, author of one of the world's leading bestsellers,

Think and Grow Rich (1965) which has been studied vigorously by many successful entrepreneurs, has this to say:

> All the great leaders, in all walks of life and during all periods of history, have attained their leadership by the application of their abilities behind a definite major purpose.
>
> It is no less impressive to observe that those who are classified as failures have no such purpose, but go around and around, like a ship without a rudder, coming back always empty-handed, to their starting point.

Personally, when I spend time working on my statement of purpose it is as if I've just cleaned my dirty sunglasses. Usually we don't notice our glasses need cleaning until we can hardly see out of them. Once they're clean we wonder how we could have been so blind. By writing down my thoughts it is as if I've cleaned the windows of my mind. And every time I do it, I see things even more clearly. When we see more clearly what matters, we see things we need to change, and it becomes easier to take those first steps. Everyone I know who has done this internal audit talks glowingly and enthusiastically of increased external power.

KICKING IN TO THE POWER OF THE SUBCONSCIOUS

There is one more important point to recognise before we start writing our statement of purpose.

Visualisation and affirmation of our desired outcomes is an important success principle in learning better time management skills, or anything else for that matter. In order to change our ways of thinking — and therefore of acting — we have to *reprogramme* our subconscious. The subconscious doesn't know the difference between true and false, future and present, and it won't be changed just by wishing or wanting. There's no power in a wish, but there's a lot of power in a clear decision.

> As we study how the brain and mind work, we realize that the process of holding a dream or a vision clearly in mind is the first step toward finding the path from current reality to this new reality. We now know that neuro-chemically, when we hold an exciting or inspiring dream clearly in mind, the chemical makeup in our brain changes, which actually transforms the way we think. (McGee-Cooper & Trammell, 1994)

I would add that if we change the way we think, we *have* to change the way we act. It is impossible to do otherwise.

Learn to speak or write your desires or goals in present tense language. It's a common response, when you first start to learn about the power of the subconscious, to feel that you're telling lies to yourself when you do this. Suppose you knew you still had a way to go in developing a healthy body. You would write: 'I value health. I am physically healthy'; or, 'I care for my body, and exercise regularly'. At first when you say, 'I exercise regularly' your subconscious tells you, 'What a liar! You're doing no such thing.' If you keep on speaking your intention, however, it eventually says, 'Oh well, if you say so!' and, surprisingly quickly, changes start to take place. Change comes from the inside first, and is manifested externally last of all.

Most of us are not comfortable speaking of a future desire in the present tense. Instead we say things like: 'I want to be physically healthy. I am going to start exercising soon.'

How strong is a statement like that? Are you persuaded? If

you're not, what chance has your subconscious got? All top athletes and businesspeople know the importance of a positive mental attitude, of speaking, acting, and thinking in the present tense. What you speak, you get.

If you gag on the present tense, write down your goal the best way you can and then work on developing it into a present tense statement. Keep coming back to the exercise until you can translate it into 'now' time. For example, even though at present you can't manage three flights of stairs without puffing, you could say: 'By June I am fit enough to run for 30 minutes without stopping.'

Here are some examples of turning value words into preliminary mission statement sentences:

Value: Good attitude.
Expanding statement: I am a positive, cheerful person.

Value: Open to new knowledge.
Expanding statement: I constantly work on being the best 'me' I can be, always open and receptive to better ways of doing things.

Value: Financial security.
Expanding statement: I provide well for my family by being financially secure; *or*, I am excellent at handling my finances; *or*, I am in credit at the bank in all my accounts.

An empowering mission statement deals with both character and competence — what you want to be and what you want to do in your life. (Covey, 1994)

Exercise 4

Take some quiet time and something (paper or computer) to record your ideas, and write your personal mission statement. Just *do* it! Refer back to what you've already written about your key life areas and your values, and link everything together. Don't try this exercise with others around you — you need time for concentration and introspection, and personal space for intuition to flow. For some it will be the hardest thing you've done, but you will, I promise, be rewarded.

Here are some pointers to get you started. Focus on:

1. What you *are* or want to *be* (e.g., *Attitude:* I am a positive, cheerful person).
2. What *contribution* you would like to pass on to others (e.g., *Community:* I actively support and contribute to the community groups I belong to).
3. What you *base* your life on, or want your life to be based on (e.g., *Honesty:* I tell the truth at all times).
4. What you are already *good* at, and wish to improve on (e.g., *Parent:* I love my children and continue to improve my parenting skills).
5. What you would like to be *remembered* for (e.g., *Friends:* I give my support and love unreservedly to my close friends).
6. What you *do*, or want to *do* (e.g., *Work:* I give good value to my employer. I am learning new skills, in order to earn more money).
7. If you only had six months to live, what would you like to do most?
8. If you could do anything you chose, what would it be?

Notice the way I have written some of the explanatory phrases. It is important to make each statement positive and present tense

— for instance, 'I am' or 'I do', not 'I will' or 'I want' — as this has far more power on your subconscious.

I encourage you to keep practising, writing and rewriting, until you get a very tight, clear statement of purpose. It's much harder to make a short, clear statement, but again, this comes from doing the exercise. Start noticing the mission statements on company walls. Ask your friends who are interested in self-development if they have one, and if they'd mind sharing it with you. Over time you'll clarify your thinking about your own. These matters can't be completed in one quick session, for the mind needs time to process new ideas. I usually look at where I'm going with my life on at least an annual basis. Your holiday time is always a good time for evaluation, for your mind is fresh, rested, and objective. As you revisit your statement, you'll sometimes rewrite your hard-won words.

Here are a couple of paragraphs from other people's mission statements:

I am excited by the opportunities I have to grow and to change. I welcome new ideas, new opportunities and new circumstances that fulfill my major purpose.

I live in perfect harmony with my partner. We are a dynamic and unbeatable team, and achieve great success in all our activities.

Chapter 5

Getting a handle on *when* to do *what*

THE TYRANNY OF THE URGENT

For me 'the tyranny of the urgent' brings to mind a picture of the worst sort of nineteenth-century school teacher, waving a cane angrily at me because urgent items are waiting! For many people the phrase describes perfectly what they experience daily (without the school teacher). Merrill and Donna Douglass, in their book *Manage Your Time, Manage Your Work, Manage Yourself* (1980) had this to say:

> We live in constant tension between the urgent and the important. Our problem is that important things seldom must be done today, or even this week. Important things are seldom urgent. Urgent things, however, call for our attention — making endless demands of us, applying pressure every hour, every day.

> We seldom question urgent things, never knowing for sure whether they are really urgent or only masquerading as urgent. And sometimes we develop the habit of responding as if they were urgent when they're not. Many apparently urgent things are indeed masqueraders. What we

need is the wisdom, the courage, and discipline to do the
important things first. If we can break the tyranny of the
urgent, we can solve our time dilemma.

General Eisenhower used to tell his officers that there was an
inverse relationship between the things that were important and
the things that were only urgent. The more important an item,
the less likely it is to be urgent; and, conversely, the more urgent
an item, the less likely it is to be important.

If you can learn to deal with the important things first, you will
achieve some major benefits.

THE FOURTH RUNG OF THE LADDER — BEING PROACTIVE

People who take control of their circumstances, who attend to the
important activities instead of allowing the urgent items to
control them, are *proactive*. They don't feel out of control,
pushed and pulled by the winds of fate. For instance, if they don't
enjoy their work they will go out and find a new job; and, instead
of automatically accepting that the current way of doing things is
the best and only way, they actively look for improved methods.

A *reactive* person, on the other hand, passively accepts what
comes, even when they don't like it. They tend to feel controlled
by the urgencies of everyday life, and seem unable to reach
beyond the immediate and attend first to the actions that will
make the biggest difference.

TOOLS FOR YOUR TOOL BOX — A DIAGRAM OF THE WAY WE USE OUR TIME

Have a look at the model in Figure F. It has been recommended
in various forms by many time management writers, and is a powerful tool for breaking that urgency trap. In a very simple,

pictorial way it highlights various activities in terms of what is urgent and what is important.

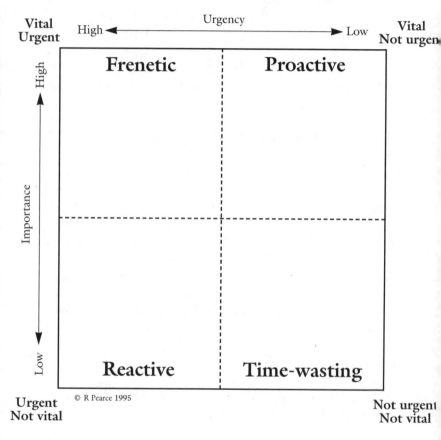

Figure F: Action Styles Diagram.

Frenetic

This category includes: any sort of deadline; crises; fire-fighting because something wasn't done properly the first time; things which haven't been planned for, or should have been planned for and weren't; things which absolutely have to be done today, otherwise you're not doing your job or being responsible.

It does not include items which have been planned and prepared for, such as appointments, meetings, or any other scheduled items.

Obviously any effective, responsible person will deal with these urgent and vital activities as they arise. They're the 'have tos' of life, and we usually wish they'd go away!

Proactive

This is the category that many people dodge around and tend to leave until last. It is, however, the power point of effective time management. Master proactivity, and you master yourself.

Included here are weekly and daily planning; forward long-term planning; preventing crises (Frenetic items); further education and study; development of new products and programmes; cultivation of new clients (every industry needs them); relationships; recreation; anything that will make a significant long-term difference in your life.

Reactive

Here we encounter interruptions and unexpected visitors; a large amount of paperwork; meetings and phone calls.

Most of us have a multitude of these items. They never go away, and we never seem to catch up. In general terms they are other people's urgencies, not our own. Most people spend 50–70 percent of their day in this category, especially with phone calls and unexpected visitors. It is very easy to fall into the trap of specialising in reactive activities.

An important distinction: If your job is to attend to other people's needs, that is *responsive* rather than reactive. Many jobs are designed to answer the needs of others: providing customer service, handling complaints, warranty work, retail, PA and receptionist work are examples. By looking for improved ways to provide their service, these people can choose to work from a proactive perspective, rather than operating from an 'I do what I'm told' mindset. And the spin-off is that, by taking an active interest in their work, they usually get promoted very quickly.

KEY POINT No. 9: Beware of majoring in minor things.

Time-wasting

These activities include: any sort of trivial time-wasters; an excessive amount of anything, such as television viewing, light reading, time at the pub, computer games, and so on; too many coffee breaks, long lunches, and other enjoyable but irrelevant little byways, such as organising office sweepstakes.

In general, this category is made up of things that, if you didn't do them, would make no difference to your life — in fact, doing them may have a negative impact because they have replaced other, more productive activities.

A CLOSER LOOK AT PROACTIVE ACTIVITY

As we've already mentioned, this is the power point of time management. The more we learn to focus on being proactive with our day, our week, and our life, the more in control we feel. The reason for working through principles, values, and mission statements before introducing you to this concept is to help you be sure that you truly know what constitutes a Proactive activity.

- How many people do you know whose focus is on proactive activities? They'll be easy to identify.
- Do *you* focus on proactive activities?

The reality is that most people spend their lives oscillating between Frenetic and Reactive, with an occasional dip into Time-wasting for light relief. Working consistently in Proactive seems like hard work.

If they could only realise the power which comes from letting go of their addiction to urgency and experience the stress-reduced living of 'proactivity', they'd never go back to their old habits.

AN INSIDIOUS ADDICTION

Did you know that many people are addicted to urgency? How familiar is the following scene?

Tom has a big project to complete. It is due in two weeks. He knows it will take about ten hours to complete. So he starts it two days before D-Day, has to take work home because of the number of inconsiderate(!) interruptions he experiences at the office, and at the last minute, under considerable pressure and stress, completes the task.

In his heart of hearts, he knows he could have done a better job if he'd started earlier, but it was as if a huge brick wall was barring the way to getting going. He always has such good intentions, but they never seem to happen.

His explanation is, 'I always work better under pressure' and 'Deadlines suit me'.

You've heard it all before, haven't you!

The truth is, Tom is actually addicted to stress and last-minute pressure. If you gave him twice as long to prepare, it would still be done at the last minute. He doesn't know how to function without pressure and is so uncomfortable without it that he wastes time instead on inconsequential time-filling activities. When the pressure comes on again the adrenalin starts to flow, his energy levels rise, and — like an alcoholic with a bottle almost within reach — he starts to move.

How do I know this scene so well? I've been there.

Until a few years ago I was the female version of Tom. However, as I developed more awareness of the benefits of operating from a proactive position, the dependence on stress, pressure, and anxiety faded. The pleasure of being on time for things and being ready in advance for events and deadlines became stronger and stronger the more I achieved it. Taking one small step at a time, I practised saying no to the old habits of last-minuting and putting myself under pressure. Now, the old comfortable habits are uncomfortable. I don't feel good when I slip up.

Every now and then, a little nasty from the past sneaks past my guard just to keep me humble. It reminds me of what it felt like to be nearly always late for everything. Over time, however, I have made most of my activities into proactive ones, and my usual Action Styles Diagram is transformed to that shown in Figure G.

I'm glad to say no-one, no matter how addicted to stress and urgency they are, has to stay in that mode. The answer is in your own hands — but more than anything, you have to *want* to change and be prepared to do something about it.

Those lucky people who have always been well organised won't understand what we're talking about but, believe me, it is a very real problem for many of us.

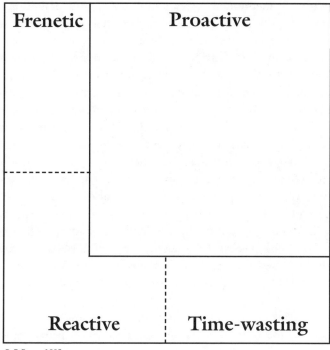

© R Pearce 1995

Figure G: The Action Styles Diagram
of a proactive person.

RECREATION

About now, I can hear you saying, 'Where is the relaxation time? This theory is all very well and good, but it sounds rather restrictive. Do you mean I can't ever blob out, if I'm going to become more effective?'

Quite the reverse, actually. Did you notice that in the Proactive category we mentioned recreation? What is your definition of recreation? Try putting a hyphen between *re* and *creation*. 'Re-creation' has a much broader meaning.

I believe that re-creation is a time when we recharge our batteries, restore our souls, *re-create* ourselves. If 'blob' time is what you need in order to achieve that, great. It is the deliberate gift of prime time to yourself, to do whatever you choose — even nothing, if that is your wish. One of my clients in the fitness industry relaxes at home with a book; others who sit at desks all day crave the wilds, the beaches or the exhilaration of sailing. One friend, who grew up in a textile manufacturing family and who loves the feel and colour of fabrics, has to do her patchwork and other sewing, or she starts to wither. Another person I knew became really grumpy if he hadn't ridden his horse for a few weeks. A few good hours on horseback and he became a different man. Each to their own — and no-one else has the right to dictate to another human being what their 'soul food' should be.

However, beware of becoming dependent on the 'plug-in drug'. Obviously there are some good television programmes, and some undemanding viewing can be very soothing at the end of a stressful day. The danger lies in taking it to excess.

> KEY POINT No. 10: Cherish your personal time. By giving quality time to yourself you have more to give to those you love.

RELATIONSHIPS
How many people do you know who work all the hours God gives them, and then wonder where their family has gone when they reach what they perceive as the pinnacle of their career? There's an old song called 'Cat's in the cradle', which tells the

story of a busy man and his little son. All through the child's growing years the father keeps fobbing the son off, saying, 'Soon I'll be home, Son, and we'll get together then.' At the end of the father's life, when his son is grown up and he himself is retired and eagerly waiting for a visit, his son says, 'Soon I'll be home, Dad, and we'll get together then.'

If you have put Family as one of your values, how much time are you spending with them? Our families are very forgiving, but don't push them to breaking point. It doesn't take a lot of time to maintain good relationships, but it does take *quality* time. Sitting in front of a TV, discussing whose turn it is to make the coffee, and telling the kids to hurry off to bed, is *not* quality time.

THE 80/20 RULE

At the turn of last century an Italian economist came up with a theory. It was named the Pareto Principle after him, but is more commonly known as the 80/20 rule. It says that 20 percent of the items we do account for 80 percent of the value in our results, while the remaining 20 percent of the value comes from 80 percent of the items.

If we own a business, 20 percent of our clients create 80 percent of the income. Conversely, 20 percent of our income is generated by 80 percent of our clients. Another angle — the clients who take 80 percent of our time will only generate 20 percent of our profit.

You can wrap the ratios around in many different ways, covering most of the areas of our lives. Consider your wardrobe. I suggest that you probably wear 20 percent of your clothes 80 percent of the time. Think of your garden. Let's assume that the flowerbeds are overgrown and the lawns look like a hay field. One task, mowing the lawns, will take only 20 percent of the time needed to get everything tidy — but it will make 80 percent of the difference.

The most important tasks in a day only take about 20 percent of our time and will make 80 percent of the difference to the smooth running of things.

If we spent only 20 percent of our time incorporating proactive activities into our lives, we would make a significant difference to our future. Many people, especially those in very reactive situations, or who work under instructions from others, may not be able to achieve this balance on a daily basis; but if, over a week, we strive for 20 percent of proactive action, 'magic' happens, and far faster than you ever thought possible. Perhaps you put some of this 20 percent into learning new skills in your own time, and at your own cost. If your present employer doesn't recognise them, another probably will, and may offer you a job with higher pay. At the very least you've made yourself more marketable.

SOME PRACTICAL EXAMPLES OF PROACTIVE ACTIVITIES:

- Company time spent brainstorming common problems to find a solution.
- Implementation of those solutions.
- Time taken to work out the necessary improvement to a regular activity that could be performed better.
- Discussing the improvement with your boss.
- Implementing the improvement, checking and modifying it as necessary.
- Delegation, in terms of coaching and upskilling people to help you, in order to free up your time for important items. (More about this in a later chapter.)
- Going straight to the heart of a task and starting with the biggest part of it, instead of constantly tidying over the surface. For example, landscaping a garden for permanent improvement (even though it will be more messy for a while)

instead of just weeding the flower beds.

- In relationships, both personal and work, time spent finding out why someone doesn't seem very happy, rather than ignoring undercurrents and hoping a difficult situation will self-correct.

- I recently heard about a teacher who makes a practice of praising every child in her room every day. By doing so, she builds up the self-esteem of her pupils and encourages the behaviour she wants them to exhibit. Result: previously difficult children are putty in her hands and she doesn't have to waste precious time on negative discipline. When I shared that with another group of teachers, one of the senior staff looked at me askance and said, 'You wouldn't have time to do that.' I somehow suspect that quite a bit of his time is spent on discipline and control.

- An accounts department of a large international company realised, while doing a 'How to Win the Paper War' course with me, that shifting a photocopier and large table into another area would create a better paper flow and a more pleasant working environment. They also realised that their archival storage had become a tip for anything people didn't want handy any more. They delegated someone with a systematic mind to sort, file and label. The rubbish has gone, and everyone knows where to place new material and where to *replace* it. Their information retrieval processes now work efficiently, instead of adding to the stress of already very busy people.

- The same company is always under huge pressure at month end, when accounts have to be closed off and data processed and relayed to the parent body in America. During a group discussion they realised that two computers were not being fully utilised. The participants also decided that each of them should give the senior accountant a breakdown of their work timetables and due dates for vital work so that a better work-flow pattern could be created. The few hours dedicated to identifying and solving these issues have had a major impact on the efficiency of the company, saving time, improving staff morale, and therefore saving the company money.

- Another of my clients, a large importing and distribution company, had the problem of staff needing to walk some distance to use the fax. At a staff meeting one of the line managers explained how a fax facility could be installed in the PCs, which meant that staff could send faxes while sitting at their desks. No-one else in the group knew anything about the possibility, and the line manager was immediately beseiged with questions.

Every company can make its workflows more efficient. Often an outsider or a new staff member can see the gaps more easily than those who have become used to that particular environment. Newcomers are usually scared to say anything in case they are regarded as upstarts, and only sometimes does the company invite an outsider to give advice. When someone says, 'You can't do that here' an outsider is quite likely to say 'Why not?' Learn to think like an outsider, to ask yourself the 'Why' and 'Why not?' questions, and don't be fobbed off with the first answers (even when they're yours!).

Learn to develop a proactive mindset. Always look for the tasks that are going to make a difference, even if only a few minutes per day. Consider how you can do them better. People in all walks of life can develop this attitude, as long as they're prepared to think and try. Don't ignore the other activities, but keep them, and the attention you give them, in a proper perspective.

KEY POINT No. 11: Learn to focus on the vital few things which will make a long-term difference.

REACTIVE VERSUS PROACTIVE

It is only when we learn to widen our vision that we move into a proactive mode. It is rare for other people to tell us we should be doing more study, more planning, more thinking, more recreation, or spending more time with our family. These are the things we have to take personal responsibility for.

Constantly ask yourself: 'Is what I'm doing right now the best use of my time?'

Chapter 6

Monthly and weekly planning — getting the wide angle

We've talked about identifying what really matters to us. We've discussed the distinctions between urgent and important. We're now going to look at monthly and weekly planning, from a different perspective. It is a form of goal-setting, as well as linking into time planning.

First, goal-setting. What I want you to focus on here is not the goal-setting which is commonly written about, and which tends to be rather linear and sequential (for example, you decide on a result, you analyse the obstacles, decide on the action steps, set time limits, and regularly do certain activities to realise the goal). This method is briefly discussed in Chapter 11.

Such goal-setting works for some and is a very successful and valid method. For people who have a very specific, focused goal to reach, such as sportspeople aiming for the Olympics, the structured method is vital — otherwise they'd never get selected. They must be totally dedicated to their training schedules and completely one-eyed about their objective. There are many excellent books which explain the process — I personally first learnt it from Brian Tracy's tapes, book and seminars (see the bibliography at the end of this book).

However, very few people wish to live constantly with the tight regime of an Olympic trialist. There is another, more relaxed way. From discussions I've had with people from many walks of life, I estimate that traditional goal-setting and time planning work for no more than a third of the population. Many people feel hemmed in by it: it is too rigid and structured for them and they find it frustrating and crushing to the spirit. Some try it for a while and then quietly drift back to the old habits of going with the flow. Others never try at all because it all seems too hard.

We are going to look at a much more flexible style of setting goals and planning time, one that works extremely well for many different personality types. This method gives us freedom of choice as to when to do what. It allows us to be open to opportunities, rather than being focused on problem-solving. It takes goal-setting out of the 'have-to-do' category and, consequently, many people find it more relaxing. It's a mixture of 'go-with-the-flow' and keeping focus. This is not to say we don't need to be disciplined about sticking to our action plans, but it does recognise that rigid adherence to a plan sometimes locks us in to struggle and activity that has ceased to be relevant. It also takes away the sense of guilt (a wasteful and unnecessary emotion) which some people have when they don't achieve everything on their action lists.

Stuart Wilde, in his book *Life Was Never Meant to be a Struggle* (1987) says:

> The struggler sees only the goal, not the path. He is trapped by his opinion of how to reach the goal. No other possibilities exist. So life moves out of his way, leaving him to operate in a barren land. The struggler is forced to head in the direction he has set for himself. Often, in his frantic effort to make his goal, he misses the

side turning that would offer simplicity or a short cut. [He]
. . . ploughs on regardless of pain and anguish or
whether his actions are appropriate or effective.

With the simple technique we're about to discuss, we proactively choose our goals (our time choices) for the month, the week, or the day, using our intuition to guide us. We are then doing something when it feels internally right. We are also working both with our subconscious, and with a universal energy (and people have different terms for what that energy is), instead of trying to do everything in our own strength.

INTUITION — ISN'T THAT A BIT AIRY-FAIRY?

Let's discuss intuition for a minute. Is it a rather suspect concept? The quick answer is no. It is now recognised as a legitimate business tool. Tony Buzan, probably the world's foremost authority on the way the brain works and how to use it, says in *The Mind Map Book* (1993):

Intuition is a much-maligned mental skill which I and neuropsychologist Michael Gelb prefer to define as a 'superlogic'. The brain uses superlogic in order to consider its vast data bank (consisting of many billions of items gained from previous experience) in relation to any decision it has to make.

In a flash the brain completes the most astounding mathematical calculations, considering trillions of possibilities and permutations, in order to arrive at a mathematically precise estimate of probable success, which might be subconsciously expressed as follows:

'Having considered the virtually infinite database of your previous life, and integrated that with the trillion items of data you have presented me with in the current decision-making situation, my current estimate of your probability of success is 83.7862 per cent.'

The result of this massive calculation registers in the brain, is translated into a biological reaction, and is interpreted by the individual as a simple 'gut feel'.

Studies at Harvard Business School have found that managers and presidents of national and multi-national organisations attributed 80 per cent of their success to acting on intuition or 'gut feel'.

In my experience intuitive focus helps to make decisions much more simple. Once you learn to use and trust it, you make fewer mistakes in judgement than when solely using the traditional logical decision-making method. It takes practice to feel confident about using your intuition, but I'm sure you will have had some experience of it. For instance, have you ever had a gut feeling that you shouldn't do something, but you've done it anyway and then regretted your action? That little inner check was your still small voice, your intuition, your superlogic, trying to guide you.

I can remember, one day, asking a question of someone. As I was about to speak my intuitive thought was: *Save the question until later*. My logical mind said: *I might forget so I'll do it now*. I asked the question, embarrassed the man in front of an associate, didn't get the response I wanted, and wished the floor could swallow me up. As soon as I'd opened my mouth I knew I'd done the wrong thing.

Since then I've trained myself not to be quite as quick to jump thoughtlessly into situations, but to do an inner mental check first. I don't always get it right, but the more I practise it the easier it becomes. It is almost like having a conversation with another person — inside your mind.

My experience as an educator has shown me that most people know much more subconsciously than they give themselves credit for. For instance, if I ask a group to discuss a particular problem and come up with solutions, instead of my always being the expert providing the answers from the front of the room, the perfect answer always comes out. And yet all the participants in the group will have chosen the course because they felt they needed to know more about the subject.

The more we learn to listen, the easier everything becomes, including our action planning.

THE FIFTH RUNG OF THE LADDER — DOING WHAT MATTERS

Here's the process, simple as it is. (I have a personal belief that we have to constantly search for the simple ways to do things. Each year that I've been working in the time management field my processes have simplified rather than becoming more complicated.)

MONTHLY PLANNING

Each month, in each of the four key areas we worked on in Chapter 3 (Self and Wellbeing; Business and Career; Home and Family; and Community and Humanity), consider what two or three main goals (or objectives) you would like to focus on, and record them.

A demonstration chart follows. Draw up an empty page in your diary (maybe the first Sunday of each month) or if you have a loose-leaf diary, create your own monthly pages.

Community & Humanity	Self & Wellbeing
Home & Family	Business & Career

Figure H: Monthly focus chart —
What I would like to achieve this month.

WEEKLY PLANNING

Let's consider the reason behind weekly planning. After all, much traditional time management teaching has an emphasis on daily planning, so why change?

When, in a beautiful garden, we look closely at one plant, the rest of the garden will only be background and slightly out of focus. If, however, we stand back and take a wide-angle view of the whole garden, we get a clearer perspective of shape, colour, and layout. And so with any other set of circumstances. When we look closely at something we cannot, at the same time, take in the wider perspective of the surroundings.

Scheduling our activities is no different. If we mainly focus on our daily scheduling, and most of the time management planners on the market do this, we're looking at what's under our nose. Daily prioritising has its place, but *be careful*. The danger is that the items on the daily list can become the tail that wags the dog, and we tend to become immersed in the urgent, always trying to achieve more, faster, better, but not getting there.

An accounts clerk in a large multi-national company was asked to check the company telephone accounts for the previous three months (and each month's account was as thick as a telephone book). He also had the normal monthly accounts to process, and he wanted to discuss extra training on improved systems with his manager, which would be of considerable benefit to both him and the company. The item he put off was the discussion on training, and yet it was going to make the greatest impact, in the long term. Having become side-tracked by the immediacy of the phone account, he was also late processing the monthly accounts. This would have had a serious impact on the cashflow of the company if a wide-awake senior hadn't observed what was happening. Our man forgot to look at the big picture for the week, and the month.

When the choices are predominantly between the reactive things under our noses and other people's schedules, we can become caught in an addictive, tail-chasing trap. When we take responsibility for long-term results and act in a proactive way, even with work which others have requested from us, we put ourselves in the driving seat. Having a weekly focus, and planning on a weekly basis, helps us to take more control of our lives. We paint the picture of our life with broader brush-strokes. This helps us to achieve the things which really matter, to escape that life-quenching sensation of always being off the mark, and it dramatically increases our personal effectiveness.

When we did our monthly planning, I suggested having two or three major goals (or objectives) for each key area. We probably won't want to work on them all every week. So what happens to the ones not chosen this week? They are there to be observed. Even though a monthly goal is not a major focus for the week, we have an awareness of it. This gives us a chance to observe our feelings about that topic objectively, and notice other points which will be of help later. When we are ready to action it the next time, we will have a sharper and clearer focus, and will therefore be more effective. Take a couple of examples:

- Suppose I wanted to send out a marketing letter to my clients, but decided to wait until next week. While I am busy with this week's activities, I will be noticing every marketing letter that comes across my desk.

- Maybe I want to start exercising more. This week my schedule is full on, with speeches and training courses, jumping on and off planes, and I don't have a chance of doing any extra exercise. By observing the reality of what is happening and noticing my thoughts and feelings in a detached way, I am more likely to plan a sensible programme next week.

When deciding what to add to the list each week, beware of one danger: don't try and bite off more than you can chew. Be realistic. Base your decision on what else is already planned for the week ahead, what appointments you already have in place, what regular commitments you have, and allow time for the unexpected. You're not trying to conquer the world in one week. You're in for the long haul. The trap that people often fall into after learning a new way of doing things is that they try and take on too much, and then give up in disappointment when they don't reach their objectives (which, in fact, were unrealistic in the first place!).

How would it feel, in a year's time, if you had achieved even half of the goals you set for yourself in each of those four key areas of your life? Would you have made significant progress in your life and with your long-term goals? Do you think some of the achievements might be things that you would, in the past, have tended to procrastinate on?

You may choose not to work on each of the four key areas each week. That's okay. It's not always possible or convenient to do so.

One word of advice — don't wait until you get to work to do your weekly planning or you'll probably never start. The day's urgencies will be waiting to throttle you as you walk in the door!

The mechanics of weekly planning

A weekly planning sheet and a filled-out example follow on pages 63 and 64 (Figures I and J). I'm assuming that you are already using some kind of diary and will use the sheets in this book as an extra tool for clarity. If you wish, you may copy them for personal use (but not for commercial gain!). Some people clip their weekly planning sheet into their dairy; those with seven-hole diary systems incorporate them into their existing system; others keep theirs in a special folder in the office.

At the beginning or end of each week set about fifteen minutes aside to plan the coming seven days. Review your monthly goals

Weekly planning sheet

WEEK ENDING _____

What is my focus for the week, in each activity area?

GOALS FOR WEEK		MONDAY	TUESDAY	WEDNESDAY	THURSDAY	FRIDAY	SATURDAY	SUNDAY
Self & Wellbeing	7							
	8							
	9							
Business & Career	10							
	11							
	12							
	1							
Home & Family	2							
	3							
	4							
Community & Humanity	5							
	6							
	7							
	8							
	9							

© R. Pearce 1996

Figure 1: Weekly planning sheet.

WEEK ENDING _____

What is my focus for the week, in each activity area?

GOALS FOR WEEK		MONDAY	TUESDAY	WEDNESDAY	THURSDAY	FRIDAY	SATURDAY	SUNDAY
Self & Wellbeing	7	Planning time! ←	Gym 6,30 7,30	Gym 6,30 7,30	Gym 6,30 7,30			
Buy Think & Grow Rich & read 15 mins per day.	8							
Gym x 3 per week	9						Gym ←	
Business & Career	10	Suppliers'/Meeting	Accountant – review systems					
Book a management course.	11	Buy Think & Grow Rich	Call travel agent arrange w/end	Phone new potential clients				
Phone 5 potential new clients.	12	Brief Janet re training		Individual staff meetings (6 x 30 mins)	Lunch with Bob – discuss marketing ideas — Marketing meeting 2.30 ←		Clean up tool shed	
Spend time with accountant reviewing our systems.	1			Southern client visits				
Home & Family	2							
Arrange a romantic weekend.	3							
Have a family scrabble night.	4	Staff meeting ↓						
Clean up the tool shed.	5							
Community & Humanity	6							
Ring Squash Club President re suggested security system.	7		Ph. Squash Club Pres.		Scrabble night with children		Dinner with Bob & Sue	
	8	Discuss w/end away with Phil		Squash club committee mtg.				
	9							

Figure J: Sample weekly planning sheet.

and reflectively consider which ones will need some attention this week. In each key area you wish to work in, aim for one or two small goals for the coming week. Think especially about what proactive activities you could do to help move the monthly goals forward. It might be something as small as making a phone call to set up an important appointment, which will in turn make a long-term difference.

Review what you've done or not done in the preceding week. You may need to reschedule some things that remain to be done. Also, notice what you *have* achieved. Tick your wins, or in some way acknowledge your achievements.

Check the appointments already scheduled in your diary for the coming week; if using the weekly planning sheet, block in scheduled appointments and regular activities you are committed to.

Now, on your weekly planning sheet, in the time that you can control, block in appointments with yourself to do the proactive activities you've just decided on (and allow plenty of uncommitted time, because things always take longer than you think).

If you are familiar with other planning systems which use a daily prioritising method, the things you've blocked in are your high priorities, either vital and urgent or vital and non-urgent. All the other things (which, if you remember our Action Styles Diagram, will be mainly reactive items), need to be listed somewhere so you don't forget them, but treat them as the less important things they really are. I put them on the back of my weekly planning sheet. You may wish to use a 'to do' list or record them in your existing diary. The most critical point is to write them somewhere safe and which you use consistently (not on notes stuck on your phone or computer!). Confusion arises from trying to carry too many details in your head, which makes you less able to think creatively.

Look at Figure J, an example of an actual planned week. You

will see that some items are appointments, and others are high priority 'to dos'. Suppose on Monday the suppliers' meeting went on longer, or you needed to prepare something for it unexpectedly. The buying of a business development book and the training of staff are both important, proactive activities that will have long-term benefits, but they can be shifted to later in the day if necessary. At that point of decision you ask yourself the key questions again: 'What is the best use of my time? What is my Number One priority? Where am I going to get the best long-term results?' We live in a permanent state of productive tension, with decisions constantly having to be made — that's what makes life interesting. How boring it would be if we knew exactly what was going to happen all week, and it went exactly to plan!

Of course the 'special time' slots with our children or partner don't have to stick rigidly to the times we've allocated. Life isn't like that, especially with children! However, the process of writing them down is a reminder. It is incredibly easy for weeks to roll by with no quality time spent with our loved ones, unless we make a deliberate decision about doing so.

You will also see that there is plenty of empty space allowed in Figure J. This gives us some flexibility to juggle our key priorities as appropriate. I find it best, when doing weekly planning, to have fewer activities scheduled at the end of the week. If things take longer, I then have some flexibility left to accommodate them.

The hard work is all done now! Once we've planned our week (and remember that it only takes about fifteen minutes a week) the daily decisions take care of themselves.

KEY POINT No.12: Keep your planning simple — clarity and effectiveness will be the result.

Chapter 7

How to use our day wisely

THE SIXTH RUNG OF THE LADDER — DAILY FOCUS

The final step in the effective use of our time is getting a clearer picture of how we use our day. The critical factor is learning to give the best part of your day to the things that really matter. How often do you arrive at work with good intentions, with an internal conversation going something like this?:

> Today I am definitely going to get started on that report for the boss. I'll book an appointment with the new member of staff, just to check that she has no problems and knows what is expected of her. And that heap of professional journals isn't getting any smaller. Jim mentioned there was a very good article on paper-handling systems, and I'm sick of my office looking like a bomb-site. I'll definitely dig that article out.

You reach your office, the phone starts ringing, there is a pile of 'stuff' still waiting to be attended to from yesterday, and two staff members are waiting to see you. You plough straight into the fray, attending to each item as it waves its hand at you, much too busy to analyse what is going on, and when the rush dies down it's 2 pm. The good intentions have become rather jaded, your energy levels have dropped to survival mode because you haven't even had time for lunch, and you've just remembered that a newsletter must be done now or the secretary won't have time to finish it today.

You may find it reassuring to know that many other people operate the same way most of the time, but I'm not encouraging you to do so! Successful people don't make a regular habit of such work patterns. They don't start with the tasks under their nose or the ones making the most noise. They don't get distracted by all the interesting, easier items that gobble up huge tracts of time. Of course, it's more fun doing the easy things, and this appeals to our desire for instant gratification. But if we're really honest with ourselves, the easy things can usually wait, can be passed on to someone else, or don't really need to be done.

Successful people plan their day. This now becomes simple and very quick, if we've already done our planning for the week. It is more of a review and overview, an opportunity for adjustment if we haven't been allocating enough time for some projects. It's also an opportunity to change appointments if something urgent has swooped in, and so on. It's time quickly to review the list of jobs, and see what to fit into today's gaps. And, because we've already got our wide-angle focus of the weekly plan in front of us, it becomes much easier to procrastinate on the time-stealers which don't really matter.

> KEY POINT No. 13: By doing the most important tasks early in the day, we experience more job satisfaction and do a better job.

Even if we only do one thing on our list, because of major interruptions, we'll still have a sense of satisfaction because we've done the most important thing.

Interruptions are easier to handle if we're working on our top priority. The feeling of self-esteem we create by starting an important task (especially if it has been pushed aside for some time), is so powerful that less important things are easily ignored.

Once the top priority things are handled, the rest of the day usually flows very easily. Even if major crises erupt, we still have a feeling of control.

PRIORITISING THE DAILY TASKS

There is a famous story that illustrates the basic method of daily prioritising. Many of the seven-ring binder diary systems teach a more complex version of this story, but why make it complicated when it can be simple? I find this method very helpful if I have many daily tasks.

In America in the 1930s the head of Bethlehem Steel, Charles Schwab, called in a management consultant named Ivy Lee as he was seeking to make his company more productive. Sources vary as to whether Mr Lee spent hours, days or weeks analysing the steel company (I suspect a bit of poetic licence has crept in over the last 60 years) but when asked for his report, he gave a very simple message.

1. Write down all the tasks you wish to do today.
2. Identify the five most important tasks, and number them in order of priority.
3. Start with No. 1, and don't leave it until you have either finished, or gone as far as you can go today. Only then allow yourself to start on the next item.
4. As extra items bounce at you throughout the day, deal with them if necessary. If not instantly urgent, add them to the list.

5. When the top five items have been completed, or taken as far as possible, repeat the prioritising process, but include the other things which have jumped onto the list during the course of the day.
6. Practise this system until you have learnt it, and then teach it to your managers.

When Schwab asked Lee how much he wished to be paid for this advice, Lee answered, 'Use it for a month, and then pay me what you think it's worth.' A month later a cheque for US$25,000 landed on Ivy Lee's desk. When asked later why he paid so much for such seemingly simple information, Mr Schwab replied that it was the single most useful piece of advice he had ever had, and he considered it significant in moving Bethlehem Steel into the premier position in the industry that it subsequently enjoyed.

If we use Ivy Lee's 'Top 5' method, the tasks on our high priority list will be attended to in the gaps between our planned and scheduled activities, and the 'must-do' interruptions that throw themselves into the ring with mad abandon. (Don't let yourself be diverted to low-priority interruptions, though. Add them to the list, and deal with them in due time.)

The two systems work together well if we do the weekly planning first. The difference between Ivy Lee's method and the weekly planning is that, through the weekly focus on our key life areas, we've already scheduled our top-priority activities into the week. All we need to do each day is prioritise the lower-value actions, many of which will be reactive items.

No item on a list can share the same priority, because although we can do several things — such as address an envelope and answer the phone — simultaneously, we can only hold one thought in our mind at a time. There may be many equally important things on our list, but we have to make a choice. The simple process of making this decision at the beginning of the day frees up our minds in a remarkably powerful way.

DIARIES

We've touched briefly on different diary systems. There are as many different types of diaries and planners on the market as there are nations of the world, and more and more computer-based systems are becoming available. For those who are serious about multiple commitments and have a very busy work schedule, I strongly recommend getting a proper planner, of which there are a number. Most of them are only available from the companies selling them, or their agents. For those who have fewer commitments, or a slimmer budget, a simple one-page-per-day diary will get you started. Unless you need a desk diary at your office for client appointments, don't fall into the trap of trying to run several diary or calendar systems — you only create confusion and extra work in having to keep them all up to date.

HIGH RETURN ACTIVITIES — WHERE DO THE BEST REWARDS COME?

In any organisation there are a few basic functions which are central to its effective functioning.

For a classroom teacher the high-return activity will be enabling the children to learn well. For a principal it will be empowering staff to be effective teachers by having a smoothly running school. For a graphic designer it will be producing good designs, within deadlines, and constantly increasing their creative ability. For a landscaper it will be building the right structures as economically as possible, and choosing the right plants for the environment. For anyone directly in sales, it is generating the sale. For management and administration executives, it is enabling the company to make a profit, otherwise eventually there will be no jobs.

KEY POINT No. 14: Identify which activities are going to give you the highest return. Ask yourself this question frequently: What is the best use of my time right now?

FINAL THOUGHTS

As I finish writing this, I am sitting looking over beautiful Lake Rotorua, having a Proactive writing time. On the wall of the Waiteti Lodge, the immaculate bed and breakfast home I'm staying in, are some words I'd like to share with you.

A Prayer for Today
This is the beginning of a new day.
God has given me this day
to use as I will.
I can waste it . . . or use it for good,
but what I do today is important
because I am exchanging
a day of my life for it!
When tomorrow comes,
this day will be gone forever,
leaving in its place something that
I have traded for it.
I want it to be gain and not loss;
good and not evil;
success and not failure;
in order that I shall not regret
the price I have paid for it.

PART
2

Now we are effective, let's be efficient

Chapter 8

Time-wasters

> Time is like a precious jewel. It must be guarded well and worn with discretion or you will suddenly realise that it has been stolen. (Bland, 1972)

In Part 1 we discussed the importance of first focusing on being *effective* — of putting our energy into the activities which will make a long-term difference. Now those foundations are laid, we can focus on the practical efficiencies which will streamline our work habits and make us more *efficient*.

In this chapter we are going to:
- identify the major time-wasters
- discuss ways to beat them
- learn to focus on proactive rather than reactive activities.

MAJOR TIME-WASTERS
1. Telephone
2. Visitors
3. Paper
4. Lack of planning
5. Fire-fighting
6. Socialising

7. Indecision
8. Perfectionism
9. TV

Remember the 80/20 rule? Here's another application: 80 percent of the most important things to be done in a day will be achieved in 20 percent of your day. So what's happening during the rest of the day? How much time can we save by looking at *how* we do *what* we do?

Time-wasters wave at us all day long. In our heart of hearts we know what they are. Problem is, often we think there's nothing we can do. In fact, there's always a solution, if you bend your mind enough to finding it.

First you need clarity of purpose, which I hope you've started developing as you worked through the previous chapters. The best tool to fight time-wasters is a firm decision to concentrate on the few things that, in a day, will make a long-term difference. Then time-wasters don't get as much chance to wreak havoc on your schedule. It's very easy to slip into time-wasting mode, for we are surrounded by people and opportunities waiting to waste our time.

Do you want to be part of the crowd, just average, or do you want to be known as an effective person who achieves results and doesn't waste time? Top achievers are people who don't waste time and are prepared to be seen as leaders in their field. Sometimes, when you first start learning about principles of effective living, it seems a lonely walk, but if you persevere it very quickly becomes richly satisfying. On the way you meet many other successful people with a similar outlook.

There are many more people happy to hang comfortably on to the shirt-tails of their old habits, to stay in their comfort zone, than there are success-minded people. Many people are unable to cope with standing out from the mass and would rather carry on the time-wasting habits of their associates. I somehow think that sort of person isn't reading this book!

We'll begin our survey of the major time-wasters with the words of Benjamin Franklin: 'Dost thou love life? Then do not squander time; for that's the stuff life is made of.'

THE TELEPHONE

For many people, this is their biggest challenge. Is it because, as children, we learnt to use it as a tool for communicating with our friends? But imagine trying to do business without it! It is both a tremendous time-saver and a tremendous time-stealer.

- Learn to control the telephone, or it will control you.
- Regard your telephone as a business tool, not a social one.
- Practise having quick, to-the-point conversations.

Don't get bogged down in social chit-chat. Listen to what you say when you start and finish business conversations. How many times do you say 'How are you' instead of 'How can I help you'? How many times have you heard yourself, at the end of a conversation, say things like 'How was your holiday?' or 'What are you doing for the weekend?' and then wished, ten minutes later, that you hadn't?

If you are the caller, you can get to the point immediately by saying, 'The purpose of my call is . . . '. The person at the other end then knows that you respect their time.

If a caller is long-winded, here are a few suggestions:

- Create a sense of urgency by using phrases such as 'I know you're busy, so I won't hold you up'; 'Before we finish, the last point is . . . '; 'I know it's not appropriate for me to take up your work time on personal chat. Let's make a date to get together after work sometime.'
- If you've finished the business and the caller has verbal diar-rhoea, a tongue-in-cheek solution is to cut yourself off. No one will ever believe that you'd cut yourself off 'accidently' in mid-sentence.
- Drop something noisily onto the floor and say, 'I'm sorry, something's fallen over. I'll have to go.'
- If you are using a mobile phone, say 'The battery's running down. I'll have to finish very soon.' (Well, it is running down if it's being used, isn't it?)

Sometimes the hardest person to train is yourself. What about keeping an egg-timer on your desk, and tipping it to 'start' when a conversation starts? Know how long it takes to run through, and develop a sense of urgency about terminating phone calls quickly.

Make a mini-agenda when placing a call, especially if you have more than one thing to discuss. Know what you're going to say, and keep notes of the conversation in your diary. How many times have you been told something, not written it down because you thought you would remember it, and then wasted time stumbling around ineffectively? If you have to leave a message for someone, make a note in your diary of why you called them. How many times has someone returned a call, and you can't remember one of the items you wanted to discuss? If you've ever heard your-self say 'I know there's something else I wanted to talk about' you'll know what I mean!

If you are ruled by the phone, you are showing lack of self-discipline or your desire to be up with the play is perhaps taking responsibility away from your staff.

If you are in a job that requires very strict concentration, such as computer programming, taking a phone call could cost you up to two hours of wasted work, because of the time needed to refocus on where you were before the interruption. You would think people in such jobs wouldn't take calls when in full concentration mode, but not necessarily so! You may have to get others to take messages for you to reduce time you waste on refocusing.

Phone calls during meetings

If someone is with you, having made an appointment, it is very discourteous to respond to the phone. The person who has taken the trouble to schedule an appointment deserves top priority, because they have treated this time as important to both of you. Taking the phone call also disrupts your focus, and causes the appointment to take longer than necessary.

- Have your calls held by the receptionist or secretary if you have one, arrange for them to be diverted to someone else's phone, use an answerphone if you are a small business or work from home, or if all else fails, take the phone off the hook.

- Consider the cost to the company of having that staff member twiddling their thumbs while you take yet another call!

- If you are having a meeting with a colleague who constantly keeps you waiting while they take calls, get up and leave the room. You may need to leave them a note that you'd like to see them when they are free. Or try saying, 'Shall I ask the receptionist to hold calls for us both?'

Avoiding unwanted calls

If you are bombarded by people you don't wish to talk to, consider having your calls screened by a receptionist or secretary. Some businesspeople are deluged by phone calls from people looking for sponsorship, people selling advertising, people looking for work, and so on. If they answered every call as it came in they wouldn't finish half their necessary work. In this type of situation, if the caller can't be identified as someone you want to talk to, don't ring them back. If the matter is truly important, they'll chase you. (Obviously, if you have a sales job, you wouldn't use this technique.) If you are self-employed, or work from home, you may find the answerphone is one of the most useful tools ever invented. It lets you be proactive instead of reactive. Think of it as an electronic secretary. If someone isn't prepared to leave a message, then it probably isn't that important anyway — the machine takes the place of the secretary doing the screening. An answerphone is useful if:

- you have an appointment with someone who is paying for your time — they certainly don't want to be interrupted.
- you need a block of time to work on a big task but don't want to lose those all-important calls.

It is very hard to not pick up a ringing phone when you're sitting beside it, because our conditioning is to respond. Try working in a room away from the phone, or turn the ring off and the machine volume right down (many modern phones will still pick up a recorded message).

Another option, especially for small businesses, is the pager. One of the advantages is that there is a real live person at the other end, instead of a machine, so you don't get the 'beeps' of people hanging up.

If you do not work at all well in close quarters with others try to do work that needs concentration away from where other staff members are talking on the phone or to other people. Alternatively, learn to switch your mind off. Different personality types handle this one in different ways. Be aware of the conditions in which you work best and try to avoid situations that put you under stress. Is it possible to do some of your work at home, away from distractions? Can you work glide time?

Batch your calls. This way you'll find you take much less time than if you had answered each one as it came in. Remember the last time you came into the office and had a batch of calls to return? You create a sense of urgency which helps you deal with them more quickly. The other benefit is that your concentration on another task has not been interrupted.

VISITORS

Before we start on skills to avoid wasting time with drop-in visitors, I do want to stress that a lot of highly important work requires you to be talking to people. The tips I'm now going to discuss may help you to be proactive, rather than reactive.

Do you actually enjoy having people drop in? Learn to enjoy it elsewhere. Meet visitors outside. Suggest lunch or a coffee somewhere else. It's more refreshing anyway, and you'll come back more focused to work.

When faced with the question: 'Have you got a minute?' don't fall into the courtesy trap of saying yes when you really want to say no. Learn to give a polite no, and then tell them when they can see you.

If your staff are used to you dropping everything whenever they put their head around your door, you will have to re-educate them. Explain that you are working on being more efficient so that you can help them more effectively. They'll be pleased with the improved efficiency once they get used to the new regime. A spin-off is that at least half the problems they think they need your help on will be solved before they reach you.

A complete open-door policy, which has been a popular management technique for some years, is not conducive to good time management. As long as the staff have been properly trained (more on this in the chapter on Delegation) they don't need to be constantly spoonfed. It is also a better use of time for their managers to have at least one or two hours in the day when they can work without interruption. Managers who find it hard to accept that they are not indispensable only delude themselves. As Michael Gerber emphasises in his bestselling business management book *The E Myth: why most small businesses don't work and what to do about it* (1986) a successful company must be able to run effectively without the boss always present.

If you see a long-winded visitor coming, and you don't want them to settle into a long chat, stand up when they come in and go to meet them (as if you were about to go out of the room). If they sit down, it is often much harder to dislodge them.

Try some of these techniques if a visitor overstays their time:

- At the finish of business, stand up.
- Let the visitor see you looking at your watch. Say, 'I'm sorry, I will have to finish this meeting in . . . minutes. I have another appointment.' Even if the appointment is with yourself, it is still true.
- Walk a visitor to the door, saying 'I'll walk with you out to reception. I have to see . . . ', or 'I'll discuss this last point as I come with you to the lift.'

If you regularly have unwelcome visitors who don't get the hint:

- Take the visitor's chair out of your room.
- If necessary, don't make eye-contact with the chatty one. Keep your head down and continue working. Say something like: 'I'm sorry I haven't got time to stop just now. I've got a tight schedule on this one.'

- Perhaps the would-be visitor is lonely, or unhappy in their own work situation. What about scheduling a time to get together, outside of work time, and give them your full attention? They might just need a friend, but don't know how to ask.
- Shut the door, or put up a 'Do Not Disturb' sign.

If you have a secretary, educate them to act as your assistant and to block unnecessary interruptions. A good secretary should be able to get into your rhythm, and anticipate your needs. You can train him or her to interrupt you with a reminder about an imaginary appointment if a visitor has been with you longer than a pre-arranged time.

If you have to share office space and you find someone else's visitors are a problem, constructive conversation with the other person is the first step. Maybe they don't realise how disruptive you find it.

Instead of using 'you' language such as 'Your visitors talk too loudly (or too long) or . . . ', try 'I' language, e.g. 'I wonder if you could help me. I have a challenge with being able to concentrate when some of your visitors come in. I wonder if we can find a solution which will suit everyone.'

When discussing such problems, always look for a way to take responsibility. You disarm the other person by giving them emotional and mental space to be able to hear what you're saying, and they don't feel they are being accused or blamed. When we feel accused, we respond by being defensive or we fight back.

One solution to shared office challenges is to put a humorous sign on the back of your chair when you need to concentrate. It might be 'Beware, brain at work', or some message that visitors can readily interpret as 'Quiet please'. Another solution is to wear headphones when concentrating. You may choose to listen to non-intrusive music, and it gives a visual message to others that you do not wish to be disturbed.

A recent report by University of Illinois researchers found that listening to music of their choice through headphones improved the work performance of many of the office staff in a large retail firm.

The telephone and other people (drop-in visitors and chatty co-workers) are the major time-wasters for most of us, but there are various other factors which we'll now quickly consider.

MOVEMENT OF PAPER

> Computer printers produce over two and a half million pieces of paper every minute throughout the world.
> (Treacy, 1991)

We are in the information age, and often feel absolutely bombarded by written information. Since the 1970s management experts have been promising a paperless office, because of the wonders of modern computer science. What a joke!

Do you know anyone with a computer who isn't producing more paper, rather than less? The potential to reduce is there, but only a few rare people and companies have either good enough systems or sufficient faith in the technology to practise relatively paperless living. Maybe the paperless office will come, but in the meantime let's think about some practical techniques to handle those dead trees all over our desks.

A more comprehensive coverage on paper-handling techniques can be found in Chapter 13. This chapter simply offers a few quick points on paper as a time-waster.

- Try, where possible, to make a decision about each piece of paper when you first handle it.
- Don't handle your daily mail until you are ready to deal with

it properly. If you take a quick look and then go back to it later, you've just doubled those minutes and delayed work on the task in front of you.

- Some items will have to go in an 'action later' file, and be handled again. If we were to strictly adhere to the old adage 'handle each piece of paper only once' we would end up not achieving half the things we should be doing. We'd be spending excessive time in the Reactive category. The problem comes when you keep picking up pieces of paper because you are delaying the decision. Every time you handle something again you increase your distraction time.

Declan Treacy, author of *Clear Your Desk* (1991), ran a survey of 1,000 British office workers. They showed an average of more than five hours each per week spent on fire-fighting because of paperwork ineffectively dealt with the first time around.

- What is coming across your desk that you don't really need? Can some of it be passed on to others? Can some of it be cancelled at its source?
- Learn to read selectively.
- Learn to throw out what you probably won't need.
- Consider the feeling you have when you approach your desk. Does it energise you or drain you?

LACK OF PLANNING

Think back to the last time you didn't plan something properly and tried to wing it. Sometimes it works, doesn't it? But isn't there generally a nagging thought at the back of your mind that if you'd planned things better you would have had a better outcome? In the words of Lewis Carroll, 'When you don't know where you're going, any road may take you there.' Recognize that planning takes time, but saves time in the end. Sometimes we have to slow down, in order to go faster!

Sometimes when I tell people what kind of work I do, they launch into a justification for not planning. I remember a printer saying defensively, 'I haven't got time to worry about daily planning. There's just too much going on, and it all has to be done. Time management — that's for other people.' I wonder if she's still in business? You could see the stress and tension written all over her. She certainly hadn't spent any significant time in Proactive activities; her life was obviously very pressured, swinging madly between Frenetic and Reactive. There's no point in winning the battle, if you lose the war, or to put it another way — what price daily accomplishment if you lose your health, your family and your peace of mind? I felt sorry for her and I hope that someone has been able to help her see what she's doing to herself. For it's when we take time to step back slightly and get a wider and more objective view of what is going on that we realise there are always other ways of doing things.

KEY POINT No. 15: By failing to plan you are planning to fail.

I like the word 'paradigm' (pronounced *para-dime*). It is a Greek word which means example or model. It is very easy to get stuck in old paradigms (or models) of thinking, and believe that we have no alternatives. When we talk about shifting our paradigms, we are considering the possibility of other ways of looking at a situation, of finding new models or patterns of thought. The printer, stuck in her old way of thinking, completely discounted time management as something she might find useful. An open-minded person in a similar situation would have been prepared to consider that there may be other ways of looking at things: they would have been prepared to consider a 'paradigm shift'.

The best-known example of inability to shift paradigms is the

Swiss watch-making industry. It was a Swiss person who invented the digital watch system, took it to the major Swiss manufacturers, and was told: 'Why would we want to be bothered with a different way to tell the time? We are the best in the world [and they were then]. We don't need you and your invention.' So the inventor took a stand at the next Swiss Watch Fair. Who should go past but a bright-eyed entrepreneurial Japanese person. The rest is history. Even though there is now a swing again to analogue watches, look at the names of the manufacturers. By 1978 the Swiss had only 10 percent of the market share, and are only starting to recover now because a brash, entrepreneurial, visionary Swiss man called Ernst Thomke went outside the paradigms again and invented the Swatch watch (against a lot of opposition from the traditional master craftspeople of his country).

Just reading this book isn't going to get you out of the old paradigms or make you good at planning. You have to practise, practise, practise, make mistakes, and start over again. It doesn't matter if you stuff up. Everyone does! What makes a difference is what you do next. Winners learn from their mistakes, self-correct, and get back to the discipline of 'one day at a time' practising the necessary habits. I used to be very bad at time management. I went on lots of courses, and read many books to try to help myself. It took me some years to self-correct my time usage habits, and occasionally I still let myself down. But what I do is acknowledge the mistake, evaluate what could have been done better, and get on with being positive. Nothing is ever gained by beating up on yourself and giving up on new habits you're trying to learn.

One week after our first session on some basic planning techniques, a group of senior executives in a large exporting company were giving me excuses as to why they had not done the weekly planning. One of their group, a very organised and efficient person, supported me. He quietly said, 'I've used a similar system for a long time. I, too, used to have trouble, but I made myself stick to practising this planning stuff. I assure you that I could not achieve anything like as much as I do if I hadn't persevered. It wasn't always easy, but the effort has been rewarded many times over.' I then had them take fifteen minutes and complete their weekly planning for the coming week, and lights started to come on. It really wasn't so very difficult — the hardest bit was the thinking about it!

> KEY POINT No. 16: If you stuff up, don't beat up. Just get up and try again. Success comes to those with the most failures, because you cannot succeed without practice, and if you are practising you will inevitably have some failures.

People who say, 'I'm successful without having to plan. I still achieve plenty' might be even more successful if they did plan. Their success is often in spite of, not because of, their lack of planning.

FIRE-FIGHTING

If you've done your planning and spent time in the Proactive category, you should have very few fires to fight. The best way to avoid these crises is to anticipate them.

Common reasons for fire-fighting are lack of planning, unrealistic time frames, problem orientation instead of opportunity orientation, a reluctance by subordinates to break bad news, either because they don't know that you really need a rapid flow of information, or because you've bitten their head off in the past.

Here are some tips to help you deal with the situation:

1. Firstly, take time to think. Don't rush in until you've considered the possibilities and options open to you.

2. Ask questions. What is the real problem? Where possible, get input from more than one source.
3. What can you ask others to help with? Don't try to be super-human and solve all the problems singlehandedly.
4. Once you've made a decision, get on with it. Whoever hesitates is lost!
5. What can be done to avoid the same problem happening again?

SOCIALISING

A lot of time can be wasted socialising. Have you ever been in the office of commission salespeople? When I worked in real estate I noticed that, in every office, there were always some people who had very extended tea-breaks, regular social lunch-hours, and lots of chats in the corridors. Funnily enough, they were the ones who made the least money.

If you find yourself doing too much socialising at work, ask yourself: 'Is this what I'm being paid to do?' If you're self-employed or on commission, ask yourself: 'How much am I earning right now?'

Once again, the overriding question for us all is: 'What is the most valuable use of my time, right now?'

You'll enjoy your socialising more if you do it outside of work time. You'll also make more money if you're self-employed, or have happier employers. Try thinking of yourself as self-employed and head of your own corporation. If you receive a salary from someone, think of them as your No. 1 client. As we take responsibility for ourselves and develop a self-directed attitude, we find ourselves looking for opportunities for advancement instead of passively accepting what life (and the boss) dish out.

INDECISION

Most indecision is caused by ignorance, fear, or lack of confidence in the facts. Improve your fact-finding procedures, and learn to listen to your intuition. If you have to make a decision, ask yourself:

- What result do I want?
- What benefits are there in each of the possible options?
- What can go wrong?
- What other ways are there of achieving the same result?
- What other information do I need before I can make this decision?
- Who do I need to speak to in order to get that information?
- What is my gut instinct here?

Still confused? A very easy way to get clarity is to create a plus and minus balance sheet. It is sometimes called a Franklin Close.

Example: Should I look for a new job?

Plus	*Minus*
1. I'm bored with what I do, and a new job will bring new challenges.	1. I will lose my current security.
2. I'm not fulfilling my potential.	2. I like the people I work with.
3. I will probably be able to get higher pay because I have new skills and the current company hasn't given me a rise for two years.	3. It's close to home.
4. I can work longer hours now because my children don't need to be driven around any more.	

Conclusion: It might be scary, but it's time to move out of my comfort zone.

LATERAL THINKING IN DECISION-MAKING

Have you heard of lateral thinking? It's a bit like paradigm-shifting. It helps us to think 'outside the square' about an issue. The 'father' of lateral thinking is Edward de Bono. You may be interested in studying his work *Six Thinking Hats* (1992), in which he presents a very clear method of clarifying our thoughts on any issue. It involves mentally putting on one 'coloured hat' at a time, and considering the question under review only from that perspective. We may not pass on to another style of thinking until we have gone as far as we can with the hat in use. Then we move on to another colour.

White hat:	Information. What are the facts?
Red hat:	Feelings. What do I feel about this?
Black hat:	Judgment. What is wrong with this?
Yellow hat:	Benefits. What are the good points?
Blue hat:	Thinking. What thinking is needed?
Green hat:	Creativity. What new ideas are possible?

As with planning, the process of focused consideration clears the brain and helps us see the real issues much more quickly than when we turn things over and over in our minds. If we can learn to make decisions quickly, we save time.

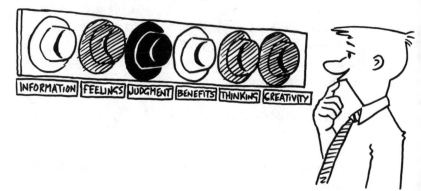

DOES IT REALLY MATTER WHAT WE DECIDE?

Successful people make decisions quickly. They're not necessarily always right, but they do decide. According to Canadian management specialist Brian Tracy, about 80 percent of all decisions should be made on the spot. Often it doesn't matter what the decision is, as long as one is made. Insistence on having all the facts first can dramatically slow up results. Use mistakes as a learning process. Accept risks as inevitable — within the parameters of common sense, obviously.

Some people find it hard to make quick decisions. They need all the data before they feel comfortable; they double-check every detail before they feel able to recommend any course of action. They hate being wrong or even possibly wrong. They make great accountants and lawyers. Try to avoid having them in company roles which need quick decision-making skills. If you are one of these people, learn to listen to your intuition. Practise quick decision-making in small things, like what meal to have at a restaurant. You might get to like it eventually! (See Chapter 10 for more about personality types.)

If you haven't got good fact-finding processes in your company, try to institute some. If you've got some good ideas, present them to your boss. Maybe ask for the subject to be put on the agenda for a staff meeting. If you're the boss, listen to what your staff are saying. They probably want the same objectives as you do — an effective, smoothly functioning company. Be open-minded. Maybe you'll find paradigm-shifting is fun!

One place in which I worked had a rule that every time a client asked the price of a particular product that was outside the normal price-range, we had to find it out from our boss. It was very frustrating and time-wasting, especially if the boss had left for the day. After I left their employment, they brought in specific guidelines. My requests for these had obviously worked, but a bit late for me!

PERFECTIONISM

> Completing low-priority tasks leads to stress, because they
> are not moving you closer to accomplishing the things that
> are important to you. (Tracy, 1991)

Be aware that if you have the bulk of a task completed, you may
not need to complete it to perfection. (Don't fall into the trap of
never completing something, however. And it doesn't mean that
you don't have to put things away when you've finished with
them, either.)

Ask yourself, and if necessary ask the boss, 'How much do I
have to do on this task to achieve the desired results?' Make that
your standard and apply it to the task in hand. For instance, can a
memo be handwritten instead of typed? Can this report be stapled
instead of expensively bound? Can a quick reply to this letter be
handwritten on the bottom of the page, photocopied and sent
back?

If you have been trained in a field which requires a high degree
of accuracy, you may have to retrain yourself not to fiddle around
crossing every *t* and dotting every *i* in a less exacting job. Each
time you catch yourself tidying up the loose ends, think: 'Is this
necessary, or am I indulging myself?'. In your heart you will
know.

If you often catch yourself saying, 'I'll just catch up with this
paperwork, and then I'll start on that pile of big tasks', beware.
You are probably majoring in minor things, focusing on perfectionism where it doesn't matter, instead of where it does.

You may also find yourself majoring in minor things if you're
not prioritising, not setting goals, or don't have enough to do
(heaven help us!). I like the comparison between the person on
holiday writing a letter to a friend, and the busy executive getting

a letter out to a supplier. The holidaymaker can spend all day deciding what to write; whether she'll sit in the sun or at the kitchen table, finding the paper, hunting for the address, writing the letter, taking it to the post-office, deciding whether to send it fast-post or standard-post, and getting back to the motel. The executive, if she is using her secretary, can deal with the matter within five minutes, apart from whatever planning time she needs to decide her response.

Again: 'What is the best use of my time right now?'

Perfectionists sometimes refuse, or seem unable, to delegate. What about the parent who says, 'I can't leave Johnny to clean up the kitchen after tea — he never does it properly, and anyway I can do it so much faster.' I'm sure you know many, many parents who fall right into that particular trap. Johnny isn't stupid; his parents are! They obviously don't realise they'll be cleaning up after him in some form or other all their lives, unless they teach him to be responsible. There are many managers who also fall into the same trap.

KEY POINT No. 17: The worst use of time is to be doing very well what need not be done at all.

TELEVISION

Of course there are some wonderful television programmes, but most of us acknowledge that it can be a huge time-waster, too. It is a very insidious thief of time.

An unbalanced diet of too much blob time in front of TV makes you passive, unmotivated, apathetic, and ineffective. The key question to ask is: 'What benefit will this programme be to me?' If you've chosen to have some recreation, that's okay. If you really should be doing something else, you are wasting your time.

KEY POINT No. 18: Any activity which is not, in some way, moving you in the direction you wish to go is a time-wasting activity. Learn to focus on your highest priority activities, and you will crowd out potential time-wasters.

Chapter 9

Meetings — unnecessary chit-chat or great business synergy?

> Good meetings create synergy; they're indispensable to healthy business. (Bozek, 1991)

For me, synergy is the combined effort of two or more people focusing on a common purpose, which is exponentially more powerful and effective than each individual's independent effort. However, many people put meetings at the top of their hit list of major time-wasters. They are an essential part of business life, but studies show some horrifying statistics. CEOs spend an average 69 percent of their time in meetings, the average person spends three to five years of their life in meetings, and about 50 percent of the time is wasted! (Bozek, 1991).

- How many meetings do you attend every month?
- How many hours do they take out of your life? Are they productive hours, or do you spend most of the time wishing you weren't there?
- Has it ever occurred to you that probably most of the other participants also wish the meetings were more productive?

WHY DO WE HAVE MEETINGS?

In his book *The Effective Executive* (1966), management writer Peter Drucker says: 'One either meets or one works — one cannot do both at the same time.' While this is a very pessimistic view, it does highlight a common perception about meetings. Focusing on the following points may help you get better value from the time you spend in meetings.

- What is the purpose of the meeting?
- Do you really need it? Are there other ways you could achieve the same results, without taking everyone away from their work to sit round a table? Could you use a questionaire, some phone calls, a short memo, have some brief one-on-one conversations, or put a poster up in a central place?
- Only invite those who need to be there. Why waste the time of people whose input won't be needed on this occasion, even if they normally attend?
- Are you having a meeting because you don't want to take responsibility for a decision (even though it's your job)? Learn to be a better decision-maker. Don't be scared. Even if you haven't got all the facts, it's likely you'll make the right decision — and if you don't, it's a learning experience.
- What about scheduling one-on-one weekly meetings between each member of staff and the person they report to? This will give both the staff member and the manager an opportunity to air their agendas. Managers — make sure you don't monopolise the meeting. Expect your staff to come with their questions and possible solutions, and be prepared to give them your time. If they raise questions on other days, ask them if they can wait until the meeting. (If the matter is immediately important, obviously you'll have to deal with it when it comes up.)

    This idea will only work if both parties are committed to

keeping this weekly appointment and not letting anything except major emergencies interfere.

The staff of one of my major clients are using the one-on-one system and have found that spontaneous interruptions between manager and staff member are significantly reduced. Also, the weekly group staff meeting is now much shorter and relevant to everybody present. The staff are much happier because they are getting personal attention and a chance to discuss their questions with the person who can give the best help.

If as a manager you think you are too busy to do this, perhaps you've forgotten that managing (helping) people is part of your job. The best testimonial any manager could want is an effective team — and if you haven't got one you're probably flat out doing their work.

OKAY PEOPLE... FIRST ITEM FOR DISCUSSION — "DO WE REALLY NEED THIS MEETING?"

Let's now look at some basic guidelines for group meetings.

AGENDA
1. Have an agenda, which everyone should be able to contribute to, circulated at least a few days before the meeting. The

benefit of this is that there are no hidden surprises, no sudden dumping of issues. When people are unprepared there is a much higher likelihood of misunderstandings and dissension.

2. The purpose of an agenda is to inform people of what will be discussed, why it will be discussed, and what you want to achieve.

   If people know before they arrive what is to be discussed, they can be prepared. This will go a long way to avoiding inefficient, unproductive meetings.

   Never assume, however, that people will come prepared. Tell them what you want them to bring and what contributions you want from them.

3. Don't allow written reports to be read out at the meeting. Circulate them beforehand or with the minutes. Discuss only the vital parts of reports.

4. Place the most important items at the top of the agenda. Then if someone has to leave early, the critical items will have been discussed. Without prioritising the agenda items, it is very easy to spend half an hour at the start on something like whether to have a staff party, and finding there are only ten minutes left to discuss spending $100,000 on new equipment because it's getting late or the key person has to leave.

5. Where possible, get closure on each item. What's the point of having another meeting if agreement can be reached now? At the very least, make sure there is some progress.

6. Be structured. Don't dodge all around the agenda. Think how a court of law runs. What would happen if they had some general discussion, some defence witnesses, some prosecution witnesses, more generalities, dodged back to an earlier witness, and so on? Confusion and mayhem! Stay focused on one issue at a time, finish that issue, and then move on.

   If you can get hold of it, watch the training video from

Video Arts called *Meetings, Bloody Meetings* starring John Cleese. If that doesn't shake up your perceptions, nothing will!

7. Give trivia the time it deserves. If an item is urgent, but relatively unimportant, put a time limit on discussion.

TIME

1. Have a definite start time, and start on time.

    The organised people who arrive on time should not be made to suffer for the slackness of others. If someone comes late, don't stop and recap — it is the latecomer's responsibility to catch up after the meeting, or from the minutes. Their tardiness expresses their disregard for the importance of other people's time. If the chairperson is regularly late, one of the other officers can begin (the chairperson will soon cotton on!).

    Some managers won't allow latecomers into the room. The sense of embarrassment about being shut out is often enough to fix bad habits. (I had it done to me once — I know!)

2. Set a finish time, and stick to it. Tell people when the meeting will finish before they come. Plan to finish by lunchtime, or the end of the working day. This reduces the temptation to overrun.

    With this system, people can plan their next appointment with confidence. Of course vital items may sometimes cause an overrun, but if they have been placed at the top of the agenda, this should be rare.

3. Try to avoid long meetings in the morning. Most people are more productive then, and if the first few hours are spent in meetings they may never really get on top of the day.

4. Encourage people to leave straight after the meeting. It keeps the momentum of the day going.

5. Don't waste the time of the whole group on something which can be easily handled by a subcommittee of two or three. If ten people each speak for two minutes, twenty minutes have gone for ever!

6. Time-saving tip — to be used with discretion. Take along other work that you can do with half an ear tuned to the meeting, and contribute when your bit comes up. (I know of at least one politician who regularly does this, and if I had to attend as many meetings as she does I might be tempted to copy her example!)

7. How about a stand-up meeting — especially if there are only a few things to sort out. When we get comfortable, we usually take longer. The sales staff of one of my clients regularly have morning stand-up meetings and get through their agenda very quickly.

GENERAL POINTS

1. If you don't know the purpose of a meeting, find out. If the chairperson hasn't yet learnt to inform attendees in advance, you can be proactive about it. Find out what you need to prepare for, and what you need to bring to the meeting to help make it successful for all concerned. Be prepared to contribute. If you go along with the mindset 'not another boring meeting', you might as well not be there.

2. If meetings you attend are not well run, what are you doing about it? Bring it up as an agenda item. Again, be proactive — don't moan and assume that someone else will fix things.

3. Before your next meeting, review the minutes to be sure you've done what you said you would.

KEY POINT No. 19: Keep practising. A well-run meeting is a work of art.

Chapter 10

Delegation — the art of gaining time by effectively involving others

Delegation is one of the main keys to improved time management. In this chapter we're going to look at eight elements for effective delegation. They are:

1. Understanding the benefits of delegation.
2. Identifying the barriers to delegation.
3. The keys to good delegation.
4. What can you delegate?
5. When you're the one being delegated to.
6. Upward delegation — watching out for other people's monkeys.
7. Sharing responsibility responsibly.
8. Personality types and how they relate to delegation.

THE BENEFITS OF DELEGATION

I'm sure Mark Twain believed in delegation. He said, 'To be good is noble, but to teach others how to be good is nobler . . . and much less trouble.' He even had Tom Sawyer demonstrate the point, in his book of the same name. Do you remember when Tom had to whitewash Aunt Polly's picket fence? His friends wanted him to play. So he tricked them into believing that only the lucky ones would be allowed to partake in the wonderful sport of fence painting. Tom got to supervise while all his mates did the painting. What a master of delegation!

If you can master this skill you will dramatically increase your work output. Your output changes from what you can do to what you can control. Good delegators give their subordinates as much responsibility and authority as they are able to accept but at the same time maintain control. Paradoxically, good delegators increase their own power by sharing it with others.

Delegation is a high-performance leadership style that produces long-term results. It helps you to build a cohesive team and allows your colleagues room to grow professionally. It increases your people skills, by forcing you to learn more about effective communication. Surveys of successful managers show that 84 percent consider effective communication at work was the most important factor in their success (Tracy, 1991).

It also forces you to be more organised. You need to be able to outline projects, assign responsibilities to the people best able to handle them, set deadlines, and check results.

Above all, delegating frees you to be more productive and creative with your time.

The largest top-soil company in my city is owned by a man who left school at fifteen, unable to read. He started his own business laying lawns with a shovel and a barrow. Only when he was in his thirties did doctors discover the physiological reason why he couldn't read, and the world of books opened up to him. In part, the need to delegate many tasks was forced upon him by his handicap, and it has become his greatest strength. He gives significant responsibility to his staff — more than any other business owner or manager I know. His people respond, and his business is growing exponentially. He does not abdicate — he empowers. At all times he knows exactly what is happening, but he works *on* his business, not *in* it.

BARRIERS TO DELEGATING

In spite of the advantages, many people resist learning to delegate. They have a really good selection of reasons, most of which don't stand up too well to close inspection. Are any of these familiar?

- If I want something done properly, I have to do it myself.
- I'm scared I'll lose control.
- I don't want to impose on my staff by asking them to do more work.
- I don't like asking, in case my staff don't like me.
- I'm afraid my subordinates will outshine me, and one day be promoted above me.
- I'm too busy to train staff.
- I can't trust my staff.
- We can't afford mistakes.
- I'm not very good at explaining how to do a task. It's easier to just get on and do it.
- I don't know how to delegate.
- There's no-one to delegate to. We're already short-staffed.
- Most of our decisions are made under crisis situations. I can't trust my staff to act on my behalf.

If you identify with any of these, help is at hand in the following section.

KEYS TO GOOD DELEGATION

Good delegation is a major challenge for most people. It doesn't come naturally — we have to learn it. We have to learn to step back and help others do the work we used to do. However, it is well worth learning to do it well.

There are various levels of delegation. The first stage is coaching, and progressively — by a process of education, supervision, and practice — true delegation (passing the whole task over) is achieved.

Before you delegate, ask yourself these questions:

- What exactly is the job? Do you understand it enough to explain it clearly? Until you can explain it clearly, you will not get good results.
- Have you got the right person for the job? Don't waste your resources trying to pick acorns off an apple tree. Don't delegate a salesperson to do the typing, or a quiet, backroom person to fill in for the receptionist. They probably won't do the job well or enjoy it, and you may all end up feeling frustrated and dissatisfied.

  Be careful of creating a staff of dead wood. Sometimes a manager finds it very difficult to remove a person from a position they've been in for a while but have proved unsuitable for. The manager then hires new staff for this job and tries to relocate the original person elsewhere within the company. If the mismatching between people and jobs continues there is a grave risk of having a mediocre company because you've made a mediocre job of choosing your staff!

Once you have chosen a suitable person:

- Carefully describe the result you want to that person.
- This is a vital step: have your chosen person explain back to you what they have understood. This step takes a few extra minutes, but often saves hours at the other end.

  One key phrase *not* to use is 'Do you understand?' No one wants to look silly. Most of us, if asked that question, will say yes. Instead, take responsibility for the possibility of miscommunication and say something like: 'In case I haven't made myself quite clear, could you tell me how you'll go about it?'

Another way could be to say: 'What would you like me to go over again?' Did you know that most of us can only hold about two or three instructions in our head at any one time, then we start to get confused. Don't explain too much at once.

If a young, not very confident staff member made a mistake I used to say it was my fault, because I obviously hadn't explained it well enough. This method takes the heat off the person you're delegating to, and they're usually quite happy to come and ask again.

- Tell your chosen person what authority or resources they have access to. If you have given them access to resources they wouldn't normally have, explain the situation to anyone else who may question the delegatee, or who needs to know.

- Tell the delegatee when the task needs to be completed by.

- If necessary, demonstrate. Then let them have a practice while you watch and guide. John Cleese, of 'Fawlty Towers' fame, is credited with the phrase (probably in one of his Video Arts training videos) 'I do it normal, I do it slow, I do it with you, and off you go'. If you start to feel impatient, just remember the first time you tried to make a computer do what you told it.

- Leave the person alone to get on with the job. There is nothing more off-putting than a boss standing over you while you're trying to practise.

One of my clients told me the story of how, when he was a student he had the chance to work for two hay-making contractors in the holidays. The first contractor told him how to drive the big unwieldy tractor and baler round the paddock, and then stood watching him, yelling every time he went even fractionally crooked. He ended up feeling really jittery and incompetent.

The second contractor explained, gave him a bit of practice while he watched, and then went away for about half an hour, saying, 'Have a practice, and then I'll come back and see how you're getting on.' Guess whom he chose to keep working for? Once he'd had some 'mistake' time, he got the hang of the technique very quickly and became very good at his job.

- Set a time to review and inspect what you have delegated. If the delegatee is inexperienced the review time might be as soon as five minutes, but it is important to give the person some time on their own.

- People who delegate commonly forget how long it took them to learn the task they're now showing someone else. Be realistic. (After all, you don't want your new staff member to be much quicker off the mark than you, do you!) You may have to show them more than once. That's okay.

- Once the person is trained, direct what needs to be done, not how it's done.

- Praise and encourage. If managers recognised the power of praise, they would always use it as a management tool. There is not enough of it in the workplace. Praise gives life, and empowers people. It gives them confidence that they are doing a good job and are appreciated.

KEY POINT No. 20: Praise releases energy, criticism kills it.

All workers, at every level, want credit and recognition for work done well. Not only does it make them feel better, they are actually able to do more. On her audio tape, *How to Present a Professional Image*, Carol Price, an American trainer on self-esteem, tells the story of a young girl working for a restaurant chain whom she encouraged to embark on a programme of thanking and acknowledging her fellow workers. This included writing them notes and sending them little cards. She was fairly new in the company — certainly not one of the management. About a year later, the company managers came to visit this particular outlet to find out why their results were consistently better than other outlets. Everything pointed to this young girl. By her positive, genuine appreciation of her colleagues, she had lifted their morale. This outflowed to the customers, who enjoyed their eating experience more, spent more money, and no doubt recommended the restaurant to others. The girl was promoted to a management position, and given a healthy pay rise.

Even one person can make a difference.

Remember: you delegate responsibility but not accountability. At the end of the day, the buck stops with the manager, even if the employee got it wrong. Almost always, I believe it is the manager's fault if there is a mistake. At some point there has been a lack of supervision or training.

WHAT CAN YOU DELEGATE?

Delegate anything that someone else can do — even only 60 percent as well as you, as long as that meets the standard required for the job. By passing a task on, you are free to work on something other people can't do. If it takes 40 percent of your day to explain, review and supervise, that still has freed up 60 percent of the time you would have otherwise spent. And the other person will improve and quickly free up more of your time, if you're teaching them correctly.

However, when you delegate, be aware of the workload of others. A lot of superiors are guilty here. Getting rid of a task may seem like efficiency to you, but if you are stressing out your staff member, you may be creating mayhem for them.

In today's business environment, many companies say they

haven't got enough people to delegate to. Occasionally that is so but often, when they look more closely, they'll find they're not using their people effectively. Staff are often under-utilised in one area and over-worked in another.

- What about bringing in part-timers, or outside contractors for some of the tasks?
- What about sending some work out?
- What about running a delegation course?

There are usually inefficiency loop-holes which can be plugged. There may be a communication block somewhere up the line. Maybe the owner or manager, bless them, hasn't learnt to let go yet. Commitment is self-generating — it cannot be forced but the fertile soil in which it grows is effective delegation. As I survey businesspeople's greatest challenges in time management, I find that as many as half of them say they do not respect their superiors' management skills. Managers desperately need to learn to delegate.

Empowered staff, who are given the opportunity to take responsibility, will almost always work to their maximum instead of working to rule. An employee who doesn't feel very important is unlikely to worry about the little time-wasters that cuddle in for comfort. However, if they feel that they 'own' their job they'll be much harder on their own time inefficiencies.

'I'VE GOT NO-ONE TO DELEGATE TO . . . '

People in small businesses often say, 'I haven't got anyone else to delegate to and I can't afford to take anyone on.' I know this feeling well — I've been there. My observation is that, generally, you need someone before you think you can quite afford them. When you reach this point, you can't afford not to have help if you're serious about moving on and being successful.

What you have to ask yourself is, 'What can I train someone else to do, and which parts can only I do?' There is a fine line here. Of course you must be mindful of the income being generated and not over-extend yourself financially to the point of risking your business. However, beware of limiting yourself by always being a small thinker — you may never have anything but a small (probably struggling) business.

Another key question to keep in mind is: 'How much can I generate per hour, and how much do I have to pay someone else per hour to do some of the tasks I'm currently doing?' Don't do work of value lower than your pay rate. Not only are you limiting yourself to low-dollar-value activity, you are also blocking yourself from progressing to higher dollar returns, simply because you can't do two things at once.

If you're not sure whether to hire someone else to help with your work, try the simple exercise below. If I hadn't done it on myself I wouldn't have hired an office manager and I wouldn't have written this book. The work only I could do and she couldn't was standing in front of a room full of people as a teacher, trainer, and facilitator, helping them learn; speaking to conferences; selling myself to potential clients; interacting with my clients in an advisory and support role; and writing. My wonderful office manager handles everything else and is kept on the run for the 30 hours a week she currently does for me. When I first wrote this chapter, I had been away from the office for the previous two-and-a-half weeks training and having a writing retreat; she had kept everything running very smoothly. She wasn't just dumped in at the deep end, though, but had been trained in all the complexities of my business over the previous six months.

1. Write down a list of all the tasks you currently do, and parts of tasks that you could train someone else to do.
2. What benefits can you see for yourself in having an assistant?

3. What will you do with the time which is freed up?
4. What impact will that have on your business and your life?
5. Now write down what stops you from hiring someone.
6. How can this be overcome?

If it is that you haven't got anyone in mind, try writing what I call a 'job description to God'. Be as detailed and specific as possible. This is not an advertisement, just a record for yourself. You might then choose to advertise, but often, if you ask around your friends and associates, you will find the perfect person for the job.

I believe that, by applying our minds to *how to fix* a problem, instead of concentrating on the problem itself, we can tap into a powerful and universal consciousness that frequently enables our desires and needs to be filled. You don't have to believe me — just try it. After all, what is the worst that can happen? No-one will know, unless you tell them! And I'm happy to promise that, if you have clarity of mind, clear focus, and a positive attitude, you will be amazed at what you will achieve.

WHEN YOU'RE BEING DELEGATED TASKS

If you're not happy with how you are delegated tasks, you may be partly at fault. Are you passive about poor delegation, unclear instructions, too much work at a time, or unclear deadlines? Here are several points to help you.

- Do you understand what is required? Repeat instructions in your own words. Don't be afraid to question. One of my students writes out the instructions she's been given whilst taking a briefing, and gets the delegator to sign.

- If you don't feel you've got the skills needed to do a task, say so and ask for help — positively. Don't wimp out and say you can't do it. Make it clear that you'd like to learn, but will need some help initially.

- Establish how much authority you have for each project. Then you don't have to keep going back to the boss for approval of each step. Make sure anyone else who needs to know about your extra authority does know.
- Where possible, when you have a problem to discuss with your boss, have some solutions to suggest. You will increase in confidence, and the boss is likely to be impressed, giving you a possible edge when promotions are being considered.
- Ask when the job needs to be completed by, and how long you have for your part.
- If the manager is one of the 'watch me while I do it' variety who doesn't understand about letting you practise, you'll have to be assertive and train them. Say nicely 'That's good. Now please may I have a turn while you watch?' Almost always they will move to one side very willingly and say, 'Oh, of course.' Use the same approach if, in a situation where someone is showing you something they're very good at and which used to be their job, old habits take over and they forget to give you a practice.
- If your manager doesn't suggest a 'review and inspect' time, tell them you want them to check you. Say when you think you'll need a review, and check when it is convenient for them. Also say that if you need help on any point you'll be asking. (Put all of this very politely and positively, of course. There are no prizes for alienating your boss!)
- Ask how perfectly the job has to be done. If it doesn't need perfection, don't get bogged down, even if you have a sense of pride in doing superb work. You're paid to produce results to the standard required.
- If your boss is a procrastinator, develop your own action plan, put it in writing, and tell them you'll be commencing by a particular time unless you hear otherwise. Most procrastinators

are delighted that someone is using their own initiative, but be sensitive as to when and with whom this is appropriate.

- If you have a manager who specialises in last-minuting, constantly loading yet another 'very urgent' job on you, ask them to prioritise the work they give you. Have a list on the wall, or written out, with the estimated amount of time each task will take. Say something like: 'These are the projects I already have on hand. Please put them in order, so I know which to attend to first.'

    When they've done so, put the list in a very visible place, and ask them to repeat the exercise each time they come in with an armload. You'll eventually train them!

    In this way you achieve two things: the boss is happy because the most urgent things are attended to, and you've put the responsibility of prioritising onto them instead of becoming a martyr to their cause.

    The unlovely cap of martyrdom fits very cosily on the heads of many willing workers, and doesn't suit them at all well. They suffer from anxiety through trying to meet all the pressures and demands. They hate saying no, and their health and personal life will suffer, too, before they finally say, 'Enough'. Then a surprised boss will say, 'You should have told me how you were feeling.' Human nature being what it is, many managerial types just keep on flogging the weary horse, until it turns around and nips!

- A delegatee receiving work from more than one person needs to have similar survival strategies. If two people you work for are contending for your time, let them slug it out between themselves. Say, very graciously (and you can't afford to have favourites in this one), 'If the two of you could please prioritise this list of work, I would really appreciate it. Then I know I'm doing the best I can for both of you.'

- As a last resort (and I'm not advocating mutiny!) don't be afraid to say no. Follow it very politely with, 'I'm sorry, but I just can't manage to fit that task in, unless I drop something off. What would you like me to leave undone?'

UPWARD DELEGATION — WATCH OUT FOR OTHER PEOPLE'S MONKEYS!

Upward delegation occurs when your subordinates have you working for them. If they keep asking for help when they could work out the answers, look out — that's a danger signal.

When they ask you to finish something for them because you know more about it than they do, or ask you to do errands as you go past, look out — that's taking up your head space on their work, not yours.

A few years ago I experienced a classic example. At the time I was president of a businesswomen's organisation and had the overall responsibility of making sure everything was ready for the monthly meeting. I had a great committee and usually everything flowed very smoothly.

The day before one of the meetings, I had a call from the woman whose job it was to organise the raffle. She is a very effective real estate salesperson, but always in a tearing hurry, whipping up a whirlwind of activity wherever she goes. The conversation went something like this.

'Oh, Robyn, I haven't had time to organise the raffle this month. I've been so busy. Could you please do it for me?'

I hesitated. I could have done it, even though I was busy, and yes, it was my job to help my committee if they needed it. I almost said yes, but something made me strong. After all there were only 24 hours to go, and she should have asked me long before this. It was clearly a case of not enough forethought. I felt a bit put-upon. At the same time it flashed through my mind that if we didn't have a raffle that month it wasn't the end of the world.

To my own surprise, being a naturally helpful sort of soul, I heard myself saying, 'No, sorry . . . I'm busy, too. I'll have to get you to handle it.'

'Oh, okay,' was the resigned response.

The next evening she was brightly selling raffle tickets. 'Glad to see you could manage it,' I said.

'Oh, it was no trouble really,' she said, laughing into my face. 'But I nearly got you, didn't I!'

A lot of managers wrestle with the upward delegation problem. They say, 'I have to keep an open door — that's what I'm here for.' They feel that they're doing their job when they have 100 interruptions per hour, and then wonder why they go home frazzled. They feel it would be demotivating to shut the door, and then have to go and hide in a different office to get away from their staff! What they're really doing is allowing their staff to be mentally lazy and not take responsibility for their own actions. It's easier and quicker to go and ask the boss! Silly boss. If you keep spoonfeeding your staff, you'll stunt their development and find yourself doing their work.

If you recognise yourself in this situation try one of these ideas, or some variation on the theme.

- If there is a problem, have the staff member write it down, along with some possible solutions. Have them decide which one they think should be used. If there are any problems with implementing that solution, write those problems down. Staff are not allowed to come to you if they're not prepared to discuss solutions as well as the problem!
- I strongly recommend you get hold of the wonderful book by Kenneth Blanchard, William Oncken, Jr., and Hal Burrows: *The One Minute Manager Meets the Monkey.* You'll have the essence of it in half an hour. Once you've met their

hard-pressed manager, sitting at his desk on a Saturday and doing the work of his staff while they are out on the golf-course having a good time, you'll think very carefully before you let your staff's monkeys hop onto your back.
• Be less available to your staff. You'll still be a responsible manager if you shut your door for an hour or so every day. You'll achieve more and you'll train your staff to seek their own solutions.

The benefits of making people think about the solutions before they come to you with the problems are:
• the other person gains confidence in their own judgment (because they are almost always right when they take the time to think things through)
• you achieve more with less stress
• the company becomes more effective.

SHARING RESPONSIBILITY RESPONSIBLY

• Be prepared to delegate challenging jobs, as well as boring ones. When you give someone else the chance to learn your job, it frees you to move on to better things. If you help someone below you to be as good as yourself, you create the opportunity for further advancement for yourself. Remember that like attracts like — if you show generosity in helping other people to advance, you will be dealt with accordingly.
• Allow others the opportunity to shine and don't hog the credit. This builds team spirit and develops the self-esteem of the colleagues concerned. If people are actively involved in a project, they enjoy greater work satisfaction.
• Not everyone feels confident about handling more work. Sometimes you have to actively encourage your staff to take more responsibility and constantly reassure them that they are making the right decisions.

I remember passing on a regular task to a very capable person. For quite some time she kept asking me to check her activity, but eventually I realised I had to tactfully refuse to do so, while reassuring her that she always did an excellent job. It is a subtle time-waster to have to continually check other people's work. It was only when I analysed the situation that I realised I wasn't helping her. It was an ego trip for me and was diminishing her confidence.

- People who won't take responsibility are either lazy or need gentle encouragement. Sometimes the best solution is just to drop them in at the deep end and make them answerable for their actions (but only do that when you're quite sure they've been trained properly and can do the work).

- If you are going to give a bigger than usual task to an employee, prepare them well in advance, so they don't feel overwhelmed.

- Give colleagues an overall picture of what is required. All of us operate better when we have clarity of purpose. Show people how their efforts will contribute to the overall result.

- Allow 'cushions of time' so that if something goes wrong you still have time to correct. If checkpoints are established before commencement, and the employee knows about them, the checking becomes a learning process, not a negative correction.

- Evaluate the risk of delegating. Ask yourself, 'What is the worst possible thing that can happen if I pass this job on?' If the consequences of failure are severe, either don't delegate, or establish very regular checkpoints.

The *One Minute Manager* books by Ken Blanchard et al. (1987, 1989) give some good techniques for training staff to take responsibility. Take into account the personality styles and experience of each person. The goal is to move from close supervision and training to the situation where you can pass a task over to a trusted colleague and know that they will complete any project excellently, with virtually no supervision. Be aware that this is not an instant process — such skill is made, not born! The responsibility is yours to train them well, but the benefits from doing so are enormous.

PERSONALITY TYPES AND DELEGATION

Nearly everyone wants to understand more about the personalities of themselves and those closest to them. The more we understand the characteristics of others the more likely we are to get the results we want from those at work, and the more harmonious our home environment will be. Having this understanding reduces the potential for conflict and the end result is that our time is used more effectively. Instead of spending hours each week trying to mediate, sort out conflict, and control the damage, we can get on with useful and productive activities.

Right back in AD 160 the Greek philosopher Galen was writing about four basic personality types. In the last nearly 2,000 years various analysis tools have been developed. Most are excellent, and it really depends who you learnt from as to which one you prefer.

My first introduction was to a very easy-to-understand book called *What Makes People Tick* written by Des Hunt of Adelaide and published by McGraw-Hill, Australia (1991). In it he uses bird names of Eagle, Peacock, Dove and Owl to describe the various personalities. It sorts us into the most dominant of the following traits: warm and confident; warm and shy; cool and confident; and cool and shy.

Eagle

These little charmers are cool, confident types. They are strong, dominant personalities, and usually naturally move into leadership positions. Their strength is that they work well without supervision. They don't need a lot of encouragement to perform, and are highly motivated by getting results.

One of their major weaknesses is that they're not very good listeners. They also hate having their time wasted. They tend to snap under stress, and then can't understand why others get upset. Some would call them bossy; they call it showing leadership.

If you want to get a favourable response from an Eagle, have your facts straight, get straight to the point, and for goodness' sake, don't nag!

Peacock

Someone on your staff likes being centre-stage? They enjoy fun, parties, noise, and quickly get bored if there's no-one else around? They'll almost certainly have a dominant Peacock style — the warm, confident ones of this world. Many salespeople, trainers, motivators, and entertainers fit in here. They are great people people, and others (mostly) enjoy being around them. If you've got a job requiring people skills, look for a Peacock.

They're great starters, not such good finishers. Too much detail bores them. (How many sales managers tear their hair out because their salespeople are very sloppy about filling in their paperwork accurately?) Quieter souls think they are much too loud and pushy; they think the quiet ones are boring! To get the best out of Peacocks, you must be prepared to encourage and praise them. They thrive on it. They are energised by being around others, and stressed by being on their own for too long. Don't put them in a lonely work environment — they won't be able to perform effectively. They need to know that they are appreciated and, even when in their heart of hearts they know they've done a good job, they still like to be told.

Dove

If we didn't have the peaceloving, supportive Doves, life would be pretty uncomfortable. These folk are the salt of the earth. They are warm, shy types. They enjoy being around other people, as long as they don't have to take centre stage. They like being support people. If you want someone to do something, chances are it is almost always a Dove who offers. They make great listeners and sympathisers. You'll find them in the helping roles, working as nurses, counsellors, and in support positions, for example. They are happiest when people need them. If the people around them are unhappy, they are unhappy, too.

Don't expect Doves to initiate, though. That is outside their comfort zone. They prefer not to have to speak out in public meetings. It is very easy to crush a Dove and not even realise you've done so, for they find it very uncomfortable to stick up for themselves. Managers have to be more thoughtful with their Doves than with any of their other more vocal staff.

Doves are the kindhearted souls who'll sacrifice their own needs for the last-minuting Peacock or the domineering Eagle who comes rushing in demanding something, without checking what else the Dove has to do. Doves find it hardest to say no to unreasonable demands.

Owl

You always knew owls were wise birds, didn't you! So are human Owls. Here we have the cool, shy folk. They make great accountants, lawyers, researchers, or anyone who needs to achieve a high degree of accuracy in their work. They thrive on being right. In fact, the possibility of having to pass work in without being able to check it several times is just about enough to bring on an anxiety attack. Their strength is their attention to detail.

Their weakness is they find it very hard to be decisive. Don't expect an Owl to make a quick decision — what if it was wrong!

The best way to get good results from Owls is to give them plenty of time to do a good, well-checked job. Don't expect them to be happy about a rushed job, and don't expect them to be able to make quick decisions. Give them a good briefing. Also, don't expect them to be happy in a work environment where they have to do heaps of interacting. They prefer a 'smattering of shush', so they can get on and do their job well.

We are all mixtures of these types, and most of us have two dominant styles. Only occasionally do we find someone who is so dominant in one style that the others hardly get a look-in. (We discover our style by filling in an 80-question sheet which is accessed through licensed agents.)

I have found that most companies have a predominance of Doves and Owls, which is probably just as well. You know the old saying 'too many Chiefs and not enough Indians', don't you? And fancy having a whole company of Peacocks. There'd never be any work done — they'd all be too busy chatting and having a good time!

In terms of delegation, when choosing someone for a task, think carefully about their personality type first. And if you want to get the best co-operation out of your workmates, learn the most effective way to interact with them. Work out the best way to approach them, under what conditions you'll get their best attention, and what support they need from you in order to do the best job.

Give an Owl plenty of time and detail; give a Peacock plenty of praise and interaction with others; appreciate your Doves and don't take them for granted; and never waste the time of an Eagle. Give Eagles just enough information to make a fast decision; leave out the superfluous detail, or they'll tend to snap your head off!

Chapter 11

The tightrope of procrastination — and how to keep your balance

At every course I run on time management, there are always some people who put their hands up for having indulged in this charming habit of procrastination! Those who suffer from it relate very easily to the earlier discussions about living under pressure, dashing from Frenetic to Reactive behaviour, and quietly hoping that the Proactive category items will be swallowed in quicksand because they never seem to get around to them! The sufferers of the 'Big P' always look slightly harried, as if invisible sheepdogs are nipping at their heels, pushing them into pens they don't want to be in.

However, there are times when procrastination is the right choice of action. To know when to delay, and on what to delay — that is the art of creating balance and effectiveness in our lives. This is creative procrastination and we'll come to it in the next chapter. First, however, we'll spend time considering negative procrastination.

NEGATIVE PROCRASTINATION — WHAT IS IT?

My definition of negative procrastination is the art of putting off until tomorrow that which could, and should, be done today.

If something needs doing, why leave it until another day? Will it get any easier?

Procrastination is the enemy of your success.

The following poem, written in 1917, recently passed across my desk. It applies to property investment, but the message traverses all industries and activities. The writer is unknown.

Procrastination

I hesitate to make a list
Of all the countless deals I've missed;
Bonanzas that were in my grip —
I watched them through my fingers slip;
The windfalls which I should have bought
Were lost because I overthought:
I thought of this, I thought of that,
I could have sworn I smelled a rat,
And while I thought things over twice
Another grabbed them at the price.

It seems I always hesitate,
Then make my mind up much too late.
A very cautious man am I
And that is why I never buy.

A corner here, ten acres there,
Compounding values year by year,
I chose to think and as I thought,
They bought the deals I should have bought.

The golden chances I had then
Are lost and will not come again.
Today I cannot be enticed

For everything's so overpriced.
The deals of yesteryear are dead;
The market's soft — and so's my head.

At times a teardrop drowns my eye
For deals I had, but did not buy;
And now life's saddest words I pen —
'IF ONLY I'D INVESTED THEN!'

How do you feel inside when you know you've delayed yet again on confronting something that, in your heart, you know you could have at least started? Do you feel good, effective, and pleased with yourself? The answer is 'no', isn't it? Learning to stick at a task until it's completed to the necessary standard is a mark of character.

Exercise 5

1. Write down five things that you know you're procrastinating on right now. Then number them 1–5 in order of priority.
2. Write down the last two or three important things you could have, or did, procrastinate on, but finally tackled successfully. How did you feel once the task was finished?

MAJOR REASONS FOR PROCRASTINATION

In this section we're going to come to grips with some of the major causes of procrastination and how to overcome them. By understanding why we procrastinate, we are half-way to dealing with this totally useless habit, for that is what it is. Then we'll look at some other techniques and strategies to beat procrastination.

1. Lack of ability to prioritise.
2. Lack of clear, written goals.
3. Not being a self-starter.

4. Lack of vision.
5. Environmental factors.
6. Indecision.
7. Lack of commitment.
8. Lack of motivation.
9. Mental fatigue.
10. A wonderful ability to major in minor things.
11. Fear of failure.
12. Fear of success.

DEALING WITH PROCRASTINATION

Improve your ability to prioritise
Many people do not understand the difference between the urgent and the important. Make sure that you do.

- Refresh your memory by going over the Action Styles Diagram in Chapter 5. This diagram is, in my opinion, one of the most powerful pieces of information I can give you. Draw it in your diary, memorise it, and learn to apply it every day of your life. If you use this guideline when planning your work, and teach yourself to plan on a weekly basis followed by daily review, I promise you will beat procrastination.
- Arrange tasks in order of their priority. Then the most important things will be done first. This is an amazingly powerful aid to overcoming procrastination.
- In addition, learn to say to yourself regularly (every time you feel yourself getting woolly about what you're doing): 'What is the best use of my time right now!' Develop a sense of urgency — less than 2 percent of the population have got one, and most of the others work for them!

If you find that a regular number of your top-priority tasks are someone else's top priorities instead of yours, you may be always seeking approval from someone else, instead of taking responsibility for your own actions. (Obviously, if you work for a boss, for example, you are working on the boss's priorities — but if you are an effective employee, they'll be yours as well.)

The power of written goals

I mentioned the linear method of goal-setting in Chapter 6. Some aspects of this method follow. By combining it with the intuitive approach, described earlier, to suit your needs and circumstances, you have a very potent tool.

Procrastinators are not good goal-setters. Unless we have a clear written statement and/or visual image of what we want to achieve, and when, we tend to float gently through life in a wishful haze of 'one day soon', and 'I'll get round to it later'.

Write your goals down. If there's anyone out there who has achieved great success without a clear, written strategy, give me a call — you'll be one of a very rare species! In all my years of research and reading, I have not come across anyone who achieved great success without tapping into the power of writing down and visualising their goals. The vital ingredient here is the power of focus.

One of my favourite stories about the value of setting goals and writing them down concerns a man called John Goddard. I don't even know if he's still alive, but if he is, I'd love to meet him. He decided at the age of fifteen that he was sick of listening to his relations saying, 'If I were younger I would do . . . ', or 'I wish I had done . . . when I was your age.' He wrote down all the things he had ever dreamt of doing — big and small — and came up with a list of 127 items. It was a very diverse list that included things like travelling to almost every country in the world, riding a camel, and reading the Bible from cover to cover. Years later, at the age of 61, he was interviewed. He had only nineteen goals to go, and these included landing on the moon and living to the year 2000. He had become a world-famous wildlife writer and photographer. In the course of his travels he had piloted a plane at the speed of sound, driven a submarine, descended the Nile in a canoe, and navigated the length of the Congo River, to mention a few items on his list. He believed that the most important element in his achievements had been writing down his dreams and goals, all those years ago (Canfield and Hansen, 1993).

Have deadlines for your goals. Beware, however, of being unrealistic. Working towards impossible deadlines is very demotivating, and won't help you break the procrastination habit. Break a task down to smaller, bite-sized pieces with realistic, achievable timelines. This often helps to get you started, and builds your belief that you can achieve something. Don't just work on the plan, however, or it becomes another form of procrastination. (Making a list is definitely no substitute for action!) Set target dates on each specific action. Build momentum into your expectations by planning to achieve a little more each time you work on the project.

Before you start each day, overview what you did the day before. Improvement comes from continuous review. Also, you will quickly realise if you're trying to achieve too much too quickly. Be prepared to take longer if necessary. Many people give up on goal-setting because they miss deadlines — every goal-setter has missed some! Don't give up. Just reschedule the time, or increase the activity rate and keep going.

Be clear about what you want to achieve. The best goals have a clearly defined outcome.

Beware of just doing maintenance work when you have a big project you want to complete. For instance, you may want to create a new garden while still keeping the rest of your section tidy. The temptation is to do a general tidy-up first, because you'll get a quick result. If you do, it's very likely you'll never get started on the big project because of interruptions. There is enormous satisfaction to be had if you can be self-determined enough to say no to the easy task, hurdle over it, and jump straight into the big task. Your self-esteem is enlarged because you've been strong-willed enough to make bold time choices, and the sense of forward momentum more than compensates for the short-term disorder you have to live with because you haven't done the easy 'under-your-nose' jobs.

There are parallel situations in business. Alarm bells ring when I hear someone say, 'I'm just going to tidy up my desk before I start on that big task'. I can almost guarantee that they are procrastinating because they're afraid (for one reason or another) of starting the big project. Develop the habit of moving forward on something that will in the long-term make a permanent difference. If you are a salesperson and you've got a messy desk, push the mess to one side so it doesn't distract you and spend half-an-hour doing five prospecting calls. Then go back to the easy stuff.

> KEY POINT No. 21: Don't focus on the immediate at the expense of the permanent.

Be goal-orientated, visualise your objectives. Take short cuts where appropriate. Ask yourself:
- what is the end result
- what will it look like when finished
- what are the quickest ways to achieve the required result?
Subdivide your tasks. Break each action down into its smallest action steps: every journey starts with a single step.

Be a self-starter
Some people have difficulty taking the first step from planning to

doing. The only way to overcome that problem is to start, even if it is only a small action step — just start somewhere. Once you have all the facts, get moving. If there is something that you seem unable to get to, re-examine it. Does it really have to be done? If not, cross it off the list — it is only demotivating to keep looking at it. If it is important, stop mucking around and do *something*.

If it's a work project you might get started by assembling all the necessary paperwork on your desk. Or you might tell your secretary you are not available for an hour. You may have to shift the necessary materials to a different place, or even a different room.

If you are procrastinating on getting the accounts ready for the accountant, make an appointment far enough ahead so that you have time to prepare. This will push you into preparation mode.

If you don't want to go to the dentist, don't think about the actual visit and what it entails. Just pick up the phone and make the appointment. The rest takes care of itself, once the first action is done.

A decision to get fit might be moved into action by ringing a friend and making a time to go running together.

I remember deciding, a few years ago, that I needed to have a major sort-out that involved combining the contents of two filing cabinets, and removing the smaller one. This was going to make more room in my study, and help me to be more efficient. It must be something to do with my early working years as a librarian, but I actually enjoy making my environment tidy. However, over the years I've trained myself to spend quality business hours on income-generating activities, rather than shuffling bits of paper. Therefore, I decided to treat myself to an office clean-out over the next holiday weekend. The tricky bit was that I found it very difficult to start. I would much rather have sat down and read a book. It seemed that everyone else was having a holiday, and my subconscious started to rebel.

I had to trick myself into getting started. I went into the office, pulled out files and started putting things into heaps. I made such a big mess that I knew I couldn't bear to walk past the door and look at it all weekend. And then I kept going a little longer, until I started feeling a sense of progress. Past experience told me that once I got beyond the initial pain of getting started, I would derive a lot of pleasure and satisfaction from the task. And once I'd reached that point, I knew I could trust myself to come back to it after a break.

Another name for a beginning task is a lead-in task. Don't allow yourself to procrastinate, while tricking yourself that you are working on a lead-in task. It should lead you towards completion of the task — it is a necessary step, not a delaying tactic. Visualise yourself getting the job done — you will then work faster and better. The key is how convincingly you can see yourself completing the task, and enjoying the benefits.

Visualise the completed task
A procrastinator is unable to visualise their tasks completed. If you haven't got a clear mental picture in your 'necktop computer' of what you want to achieve, you have no chance of achieving it. Every house built, every thriving business, every top sports achievement, starts in someone's mind.

Learn to visualise — it's very powerful. It is as if you are playing a video in your mind.
- Firstly, decide what you want to achieve.
- Secondly, spend a few minutes relaxing, slowing your mind down.
- Thirdly, play your Success Video on your internal TV screen. This involves using all five of your senses. In your imagination, see, smell, touch, hear, taste the project.
- Fourthly, do it daily, for about 5–10 minutes. No-one

becomes good at anything in one short burst. We don't become fit after two or three trips to the gym, or good salespeople after a couple of observations of how an experienced salesperson looks. Practice is the key ingredient to permanent success.

If you want to give an excellent presentation, visualise yourself in front of the client or group being successful. Imagine how good you'll feel when the client says yes, or when the group has adopted your ideas. See them sitting forward, interested in what you're saying, nodding their heads, being enthusiastic about your recommendations. Feel the positive atmosphere in the room.

You want to improve a relationship. See yourself talking harmoniously with the person concerned. Feel the positive flow of energy as you engage in stimulating conversation. Hear the laughter between the two of you.

If it's a sports achievement, see yourself playing perfect strokes or making top scores. Hear the crowd roar as you make a brilliant play. Feel the power pumping through your fit body.

If you can visualise success, you will be much more likely to do the work necessary. Practise visualising doing things you might otherwise postpone, and you'll find you achieve much more, with much less procrastination.

Your physical environment
There are a number of things you can do physically to overcome procrastination. The conditions you work in can aggravate your tendency to procrastinate. If you are uncomfortable, for example, too hot or too cold, you may not be able to concentrate. Try to establish what environment is best for you to achieve top productivity (and your needs may be different from the needs of those around you). Observe the noise levels, type of light, and time of day that you function best. Do you work better alone or with

others, before or after strenuous exercise, in the middle of the day or the middle of the night? Create a good work environment that encourages you to take action. Make changes as they are needed.

If you get mentally stuck and the ideas won't flow, take a short walk. It gives you a chance to clear your mind. New ideas will come from the sights, sounds and smells you experience, and you'll return much fresher to your task.

When you're doing a repetitive task over a long period, sometimes boredom can set in — you get tired of what you are doing. Take a short break; create a diversion. Set breaks in a task, so that you can enjoy a short rest. For instance, 'I'll have a coffee break after doing ten phone calls.' The promise of the coffee break makes it easier to start the task, and you'll be fresher when you go back to it.

If you're too tired to concentrate properly, have a cat-nap (if possible and appropriate), or try a short meditation exercise. Slowing your mind down to a state of deep relaxation is more restful than a sleep. Sometimes we forget to listen to what our body is trying to say. If you find yourself feeling really tired, it may be that your body is sending you a message. If, instead of fighting it, you give yourself permission to notice the tiredness, and do something about it, you recover much faster. Be aware that an overtired person is like a car with no petrol — no can go!

Acknowledging to yourself that it's okay to slow down when you are tired is important. Otherwise you'll tend to give yourself a hard time about being a slacker.

Overcoming indecision

Sometimes we dither around, not knowing which of several mutually exclusive activities to do. At this point we have to re-examine our priorities and values.

Have you ever been given an invitation to do something you'd like to do, but in your heart of hearts you know you can't fit it into your schedule? When you analyse your time commitments, you realise you have to make a choice. To make the 'right' choice you need to be able to identify your own priorities and values, which of course is what Part I of this book is about. The longer you toy with the tantalising alternatives, the longer you try to justify your choice to your conscience, the more muddled and confused you become.

There is a huge release of power once the right decision is made. You get back on track. You stop procrastinating on the activities that don't really matter. To help yourself find the 'right' decision, always ask yourself, 'Where am I going to get the best long-term results, that are congruent with my statement of purpose and values?' Learn to get ruthless with the time-stealers that want to take over your life.

Remember: every day brings good opportunities. The power is in making the *best* choices. Have role models in mind — people you admire greatly. Say to yourself: 'Would . . . spend their time on this task, if they had my goals?' Learn to listen to your intuition. Most importantly, learn to make the decision quickly. Don't vacillate. Once the decision is made, don't look back. Move on.

KEY POINT No. 22: Don't sacrifice the excellent for the good.

Reinforce your commitment
Once you've made a decision, if you share your goal with someone supportive you'll be much more likely to complete, thereby defeating your old procrastination habit. Give another person permission to monitor you, make yourself answerable to someone else, and watch how committed you'll become, not to mention the progress you'll make.

A few years ago I decided to train for a modified marathon (24 km). A number of my running friends were competing, and they challenged me to participate, but I really didn't think I could do it. However, once I'd made the decision, and shared it with them, they became a vital element in the outcome. I'm absolutely sure there was no way I would have sustained the three-month training programme without them.

Because I had given them permission to check and coach me, they had a personal interest in supporting and helping me. They were committed to my success. The combined energy, commitment and focus of all of us was enough to propel me through the old internal conversations about being (a) too slow, (b) too heavy, (c) not fit enough, and (d) not having enough time. The old excuses dropped away, powerless to stop me. I simply didn't need them any more. For that time, at least, procrastination was conquered.

The benefits to me of taking part in that race far exceeded the buzz I got from completing in a much better time than I'd estimated. At the time both my work situation and the relationship I was in were rather negative. The increase in my self-esteem, because of the trim 'me' I became, and the increased confidence because I persevered with my training, was terrific. I'm sure it was a major factor in my having enough confidence to move on to new horizons, new people, and the wonderful life I now lead.

One serious word of warning, however. Make sure that the people you share your goal with are people you trust, and who are willing to support and encourage you. There is a biblical phrase 'Don't cast your pearls before swine.' (Matthew 7:6.) Don't share your dreams and precious hopes with scoffers who will trample them into the mire and mud of their limited thinking. Such people encourage your procrastination, because they want company in their own negative pig-pens.

When you make a commitment to others, you find you'll think less about yourself, and more about them. You will find that your desire to keep the good opinion of someone you respect is more powerful than your own fears and indecisions. This attitude change helps to break the procrastination habit. When others share them, your accomplishments become all the more enjoyable.

Once you establish a habit, and 21–28 days is enough to get a base laid, it doesn't require anywhere near as much effort to keep going. The hardest part is about 3–4 days after you've started the new activity. Alerting someone else to check you at that time, before you get there and feel like giving up, is a big help to breaking through the barrier.

Building motivation

Many people procrastinate because of lack of motivation, and if you're not motivated you won't use your time well. You'll constantly find yourself spending time in the Reactive and Time-wasting activities. And it is very easy to keep spiralling downwards into more and more inefficiencies. If you're feeling down or sorry for yourself, you need to go on a self-building programme. Find positive, encouraging people to associate with. Remove yourself from regularly spending time with negative people. Your mental state, just like your body, needs to be properly fed.

Think of a lake, wrapped in the folds of the surrounding hills. It is fed by the water running off the hills after rain. It receives the little streams flowing into it and springs that bubble cleanly up nearby. Imagine another stream flowing away from this lake. If, over time, more water flows out than flows in, the lake turns into a mud-hole. So it is with our minds. Negative thought is a on our energy and our ability to function effectively. It diminishes, rather than enlarges, us. If we allow in more negative influences than positive ones, the glory of our minds also becomes a bog-hole of depression, negativity, and limited thinking.

All we have to do to change the ratios is:

- identify what is negative and what positive
- make sure that there is at least 51 percent positive input going into our heads on a daily basis. Anything above 51 percent will move us towards more power and success in our lives, slowly but surely. As we move forward, so the habit of procrastination drops away.

Getting that positive input means eliminating from our lives the things, happenings, and people who drain us. Cut down on negative reading in books, magazines and newspapers. Stop watching negative TV programmes. Don't start the day by listening to the world's disasters. Relax — if you don't hear every news programme you'll still know what's going on in the world, someone will tell you! Don't go to bed with a nightcap of the news or TV violence. Let the last thoughts of the day be positive ones. Give your subconscious mind productive challenges to work on while you are asleep. Avoid boring, whinging, negative people as if they had the plague. They have. They suffer from a deadly, life-sucking disease called 'it's not fair'. Such people do not realise that they're 100 percent responsible for changing their own circumstances.

If you work in a negative environment, or for a negative boss, get out while you still have a mind. Why give so much of your precious time — indeed, your life — to someone you neither like nor respect, or to a company you don't trust. And research has shown that happy people suffer less stress and have better health. They live longer, and have greater quality of life. So the more negative stress you live with, the shorter your life might be (Tracy, 1995). And if that isn't an important consideration about the way we use our time, what is? When people first become aware of this fact, they often say things like: 'But I don't want to lose my friends.' Relax — true friends are glad to see you get ahead and find success and happiness. As you grow so will they. And there are many more wonderful encouraging people waiting to meet you.

TELL ME AGAIN HOW WONDERFUL I AM

Overcoming mental fatigue

If you are severely depressed you need skilled help. What we are talking about in this section are those times when you feel a bit low and dispirited and can't seem to get motivated. Often these are symptoms of severe procrastination: you feel overwhelmed by the size and complexity of the task, and wish it would go away; the further behind you get, and the closer to an increasingly impossible deadline (because you've mucked around!) the more helpless you feel. The following pointers may help you to overcome those feelings when they arise.

- Prioritise. Do I need to tell you again to prioritise? *Just do it!*
- Develop new habits. This is an excellent solution but it means practising self-discipline. Don't expect an overnight cure. New habits take a long time to learn, and we can really focus on only one at a time.

  Benjamin Franklin gives us a wonderful example of the

power of surely but steadily building better habits. He was a printer, philosopher, writer, inventor, and American politician in the eighteenth century, and was sometimes called 'the wisest American'. His influence on society is still felt. Every wearer of bifocal glasses thanks him, Franklin diaries are named after him, and the plus/minus exercise described in Part I is called the Franklin Close — to mention only three examples.

In his autobiography he tells how argumentative he was as a young man. Eventually he decided that greater business and personal success would be his if he put himself on a self-improvement programme. He got a notebook, and wrote down thirteen areas of his life in which he wanted to improve. He figured that he wouldn't try to improve all areas at the same time; that one trait per week was about as much as he could handle. He was wise. None of us can cope with too much radical change. He drew up a chart, and developed a recording system which he updated daily in order to keep a check on himself. At the end of each week he stopped focusing on that week's trait and moved on to the next one. His thinking was that, even if he wasn't actively focusing on something, over a period of time he would improve on all fronts. History proved him right. So — take your time. If the slow road to continous improvement was good enough for Ben Franklin, it's good enough for us.

- Write a list of all your strengths and achievements, the good things you do for other people, the ways you contribute. For many of us feelings of depression go hand in hand with not feeling worthwhile. At these times we can judge ourselves much too harshly.

I encourage you to recognise what a great person you are. Everyone has heaps of wonderful things to offer other people, but do you recognise what yours are? Please learn to value yourself — you are a very special person, with unique skills and qualities, many of which you are so familiar with that you don't even recognise them as different from, or better than, other people.

I had a graphic illustration of this with one of my client companies. For homework, I had asked the group (who all worked in the same team) to write a list of their individual strengths and achievements. The next week one of the girls said that she hadn't been able to do the exercise. Nor had most of the rest of the group. Almost all of them, and they were mainly quiet non-assertive people, said that they found it highly uncomfortable to turn the telescope backwards and praise themselves for what they did well. They didn't think they were particularly good at anything, and kept mentioning other people who were better.

For a moment I was stumped, but inspiration struck. Focusing on one person at a time, I asked the group to tell their colleague his or her strengths, and anything else positive they wanted to share. One person wrote down the responses and gave them to the person in the 'hot seat'. It was very moving to sit and listen to the wonderful things they were saying to each other. The first few found it very difficult to receive praise, but as we continued, the squirming stopped. The result was electrifying. By the time they finished, you could feel the power, love, and care in the room.

- Take the focus off your weaknesses. Don't dwell on them in a negative way. They'll go away if they don't get enough attention. Everyone has their share, but don't focus on them as excuses — that's a sure way to wallow in procrastination. Do you want to spend your life having a pity party, or do you want to amount to something? When you're starting a new project, focusing on your weaknesses will guarantee failure.

> Believe in yourself. Capitalise on your strengths, and gradually weaknesses will fade into insignificance.

I speak from experience here. If you had told me ten years ago that I would develop a major business around time management, let alone be writing a book about it, I would have laughed very loudly! I could be guaranteed to be always last-minuting and I was usually late for everything except buses and planes!

So what happened to change things? I began in the training field by using one of my strengths — the ability I seem to have of encouraging people, in one-on-one sessions. Eventually I realised that many of my clients were asking me for help on how to handle their time. How could I, someone who used to be abysmal at time management, have that knowledge? Because, recognising that it was a weakness, I had focused on improving it. Rather than saying, 'I'm no good at handling my time — I'm always late', and negatively giving up, I went on courses, read books, and practised, practised, practised!

KEY POINT No. 23: Don't nurture your weak habits; ignore them and they will wither. Focus instead on the habits you want to develop — whatever you focus on enlarges.

- Spend some quiet time every day, just thinking. Observe the things around you. Take time to see and smell the flowers. Learn to be aware of things other than your busy-ness. Slow down and reflect on nature.
- Study something you're interested in. Develop a mindset that says: 'Today I will learn something new.' Every person you talk to, every book or magazine you pick up, has something new to offer you. Practise looking for it.
- Start something. Do something that takes initiative and imag-

ination. It is always the thinking-about-starting that bogs people down. Once you've begun, the pain vanishes and you find yourself saying, 'Why did I take so long?'

*   Finish something that you've begun, especially a Proactive activity (see Chapter 5). The power of completion is amazing. Even a very small task, once finished, causes an adrenalin flow which creates a positive feeling. Every little bit of positivity helps to break down the walls of depression.

*   Indulge your creativity. One of my clients was having trouble staying focused on the family business she helped her husband to run. She was caught up in 'ought to's' and 'shoulds', and was becoming more and more depressed. She is a very clever craftsperson who loves creating beautiful things, but she put her talent to one side out of a sense of duty. She found that giving herself permission to go back to her crafts from time to time lifted her spirits amazingly. (We all need to express our creativity in some way; repressing it for too long kills the spirit within us.) Once she recognised this and allowed herself some regular creative time, the other important activities that were going to make a long-term difference to her life didn't seem so hard. She then started to achieve in those areas again.

Don't major in minor things

Majoring in minor things is another habit of people who don't know how to prioritise. Occasionally you will find that you've done all the higher priority tasks for the day, and have time to do some 'busy' tasks. These can provide a welcome relief, a 'working break', and might include sorting the office files, clearing out the bottom drawer, or any other of the various administrative tasks that accumulate. However, if you spend time on these tasks when priority jobs are left undone, you allow procrastination to take over again. Don't be fooled by your seemingly important activities. Ask yourself honestly: 'What is the most important use of my time right now?'

Don't fear failure

Often, we fear to start something in case we fail. Procrastination is impossible when we understand both the task facing us and our fears about it, and prepare to deal with them. There are some steps we can take to overcome our fear of failure.

- Do you know what you are trying to accomplish, and why? If you do know you'll have taken a major step towards beating procrastination caused by fear.

- Thoroughly analyse the job. Take a sheet of paper, and write on one side all the reasons you have for completing it. On the other side list all the reasons you can think of for postponing it. Write down everything you can think of, and then compare the two lists. If a job is really important, you will have more reasons for doing than for delaying. Just putting all the reasons for and against down on paper will help give you the motivation to overcome your fear and commence the necessary work.

- If you come up with truly legitimate reasons for delaying a task, leave it and go on with something else. You won't be successful if you really hate a task — doing it will only cause anxiety and frustration. However, if someone else, such as your boss, asks you to do something disagreeable, do it straight away even if you'd like to postpone it. Putting it off always causes far more anxiety and stress than gritting your teeth and getting the damn job done!

- If the task is totally objectionable, the final recourse is to exit out of the situation. That could even mean leaving a job or ending a relationship. You have to make a decision based on your values and priorities, but only after careful analysis of the situation.

- Once you've taught yourself to analyse each situation, learn to study each challenge closely. It will be much easier for you to finish each job if you know more about it. Lack of knowledge causes apathy and fear, which then creates procrastination. You can conquer all if you learn more about what you have to do. If a task is worth completing, it's worth understanding.

  Research it before you start — this will help you to get going. Also, sharing knowledge with others and enlisting their help will often encourage you to persevere once you have begun.

Understanding the value of change

Some people actually fear success or completion of tasks. Why? For some, once a job is completed, their excuses for not getting on with the next thing are gone. Not everybody welcomes change. It may mean moving into a new stage in their life.

There always seems to be a risk in moving forward in life, in being exposed to change. I remember the first weekend of my step into self-employment. I suffered from anxiety attacks for the first, and hopefully last, time of my life. Change is scary! You simply don't know what's round the next corner. If this is you — take comfort. Change that you engineer, by progressively moving forward, is very positive. Look back in a year or so, and you'll realise you're not the same person you were, and wouldn't want to be. The pain of change is the pain of birth, the pain of growth. After you've deliberately stepped out for change and progress a few times you start looking for it, because you realise that unless there is change you're going backwards. Winners are prepared to live outside their comfort zones.

To be sure, change which is forced upon us, for one reason or another, is not usually much fun. However, we can transmute it to a positive outcome by looking for the positive spin-off. The former CEO of a very large national real estate chain in New Zealand told me, a year after being rather dramatically dumped, that although his experience was traumatic at the time, with hindsight he saw it as very positive. He now has a business in an allied field, has freedom of choice, a less stressful life, good income, and best of all he doesn't have to spend half of his life in interminable meetings! He could have chosen to wallow in self-pity. Full credit to him for moving on.

SOME OTHER HELPFUL TECHNIQUES AND STRATEGIES TO OVERCOME PROCRASTINATION

The best way to stop procrastination is never to start it! You can do this by planning. Few people plan for the most effective use of their time. The more time you spend on planning, the less you will need to complete the task, the better results you will get, and the more time you'll have for other things.

Have you ever seen a laser show, possibly at a big stage production, or a civic fireworks display? Think of the intensity and power with which laser beams cut through the air. They don't waver about. Learn to develop 'laser thinking' — it will save you from procrastination.

Where to start on big tasks

For many of us, it is the getting started that causes the most trouble. There are two opposite techniques for getting going:
- begin on the outside
- begin on the inside.

Different people operate in different ways, so you need to experiment to find out which way suits you best. The *outside to inside* people like to assemble everything first, and remove the small tasks from around the fringes before they start. For instance, they find it almost impossible to start a new project when their desk is messy. They need to take care that they don't fall into the trap of majoring in minor things, however. For instance, spending time doing all the trivial paperwork will just about guarantee a non-start on the big job. The distractions may have to be moved out of sight for the duration.

If they're going to clean a room, they prefer to sort out all the mess before they start the vacuum cleaner. They do the little things first and the big ones that make the significant difference last. This is the way they build momentum.

The *inside to outside* people do the big tasks first, and then tidy up the fringes (if you're lucky!).

There is no right or wrong in either of these methods, as long as the job is completed to a satisfactory standard. If you stop and think about the way you operate, you'll quickly identify which sort of person you are.

The traps to be aware of are:
- outside to inside people sometimes don't start the big task because they're so busy getting ready
- inside to outside people sometimes don't complete jobs properly, because the finishing touches don't motivate them!

Some of us just have to be really tough on ourselves, and set deadlines such as: 'Well, Robyn, you're just not going to leave the office (or go to bed, if it's a personal activity) until you've at least started on this job.' Most of us can delay with excellence! Creating momentum is a learned skill. Driving through that sense of sluggishness, forcing ourselves to take control of our will, is hard at first, but the more we do it, the better we feel, the more we increase our self-esteem, and the more successful we become. Winners are not procrastinators. (Yes, you're right, I am strongly identifying with this issue. I used to get excellent grades in Procrastination Class!)

What to start with

It is better to start with the worst, or most unpleasant, thing you have to do in the day. Often the thing that will make the most significant long-term difference in your life is the one thing you most don't want to do. A common one for salespeople is making prospecting calls. Confront it. Really, it will only take a few minutes to make a few calls to three or four new prospects, and the huge benefits to your self-esteem and energy far outweigh the discomfort. Over time, you become de-sensitised to the pain, and one day you will find that you really enjoy getting on the phone and speaking to people you don't know (or whatever it is that you find hard to do). I speak from vast experience here, too!

Develop a 'Do it now' mentality.

Rewards

Rewards are absolutely essential to drive you past the pain of learning to change habits.

They are a great ego booster and really help in the fight against procrastination. Choose a simple reward system. Try different things until you find something that really hits your hot button. It might be sleeping in on a Saturday, having a night out, giving yourself permission to sloth off for a few hours, reading a novel instead of a non-fiction book if that is a change you'll look forward to. Set a points or bonus system; give yourself points each time you achieve the specific action you are working to improve on.

One of my clients decided that she wanted to improve on her exercise programme. She set a goal to walk for about half an hour three times a week. She then drew up a habit chart (something like Benjamin Franklin's), and every time she took her walk, a star went up on the chart. At the end of each month she chose a reward, and sometimes I got included! One month we went to the movies in the middle of the afternoon. It felt so decadent, and did we enjoy it!

Two important details:

- Reward yourself only when you earn it.
- If you earn a reward, be sure to take it.

Reward systems only work if you strictly adhere to them. If you tell yourself you will stop after a certain amount of activity, or take a particular reward after achieving specific results, and then don't, the motivating power of a reward diminshes.

Remember, you're dealing with the hidden giant of your subconscious here. If you keep saying one thing and doing another, eventually your subconscious digs its stubborn heels in and says 'shove off'. You will have created an internal lack of integrity. In a humorous way, I see the subconscious as a child. Remember how we discussed positive statements of intention when we were writing our statements of purpose (the third step of the Ladder of Life)? Another word for these statements is 'affirmations'. Tell your subconscious something for long enough and it will eventually believe you. But if you don't keep your promises, even to yourself, you've got trouble! (For more about affirmations, read Shakti Gawain's *Creative Visualisation* (1979) or John Kehoe's *Mind Power* (1987).)

If you want to improve in any area it is much more effective to reward than to punish yourself. As always, it is a matter of focus. Remember, whatever you focus on expands, so if you focus on your deficiencies, that's what you'll be always aware of.

Learn to be detached

Sometimes we can be too close to a task. Get someone else to take a detached look at the situation. They will probably be able to see things you've overlooked. By explaining to someone else what your difficulties are, you'll find it easier to get a clear overview because you have had to go back to basics to explain.

Know what your deadlines are

Learn to budget time, just like any other valuable resource. Identify activities that waste time. Develop a tight schedule — this will help to prevent procrastination.

If you are focusing primarily on the 20 percent of activities that are going to make 80 percent of the difference, the less important activities will be crowded out. Leave undone those things that really didn't matter. (More about this in the chapter on Creative Procrastination.)

Work fast

Sometimes a fast tempo is essential to success. Quick action creates momentum. Do you know any highly effective person who fluffs around? I remember one man I worked for who could write reports and make decisions faster than anyone else I've ever known. He wasn't always right, but he was effective more often than not, achieved heaps, and had a lot of fun along the way. When you work at a fast rate, you have higher energy.

Time fillers

Learn to fill the small time-gaps with useful activities, i.e. writing a letter, making a phone call, or collecting the information or supplies you need to start your next major activity. Remember, work expands to fill the time available. If you make less time available you will probably eliminate all sorts of time-wasting activities, and find yourself still being just as effective, if not more.

Have you ever noticed how much work you can get through when you're about to go on holiday? Tasks that have been waiting for your attention for ages suddenly get handled. You seem to be working in overdrive. You feel powerful and effective, and time flies. You leave for your holiday feeling that you've earned it. Try creating that momentum all the time. You won't achieve it very often at first, but over time it becomes a way of life, and suddenly you find you are faster and more productive than those around you.

While you are waiting for someone to answer the phone, do something else as well. There is sure to be some piece of paper waiting for your attention, an envelope to address, or some notes to be made in your diary. You can glance over the day's action plan, and preview the next task. Highly effective people are minute conscious, not hour conscious.

It is possible to do two things at once, although you can only hold one thought in your mind at a time. If you know you are going to be doing lots of calls which don't require high level concentration (such as a ringing list for a club you belong to), look for something else you can do simultaneously. It might be folding newsletters and making routine calls. At home it might be cooking dinner and talking on the phone to a family member, if you have a portable phone. It might be ironing or folding washing and watching TV. When I was a child I taught myself to knit and read at the same time. You might say you can't do multiple tasks. I say: 'Have you tried, and persevered in your trying?'

(There is a gender difference to be aware of, however. Women will probably find it easier to do simultaneous tasks as their brains are constructed differently from men's. While most men have the ability to focus very single-mindedly on one thing at a time, try asking a man a question when he's watching TV! Women's brains, which have a different switching mechanism, make it easier for them to handle multiple tasks concurrently (Moir and Jessell, 1989).)

KEY POINT No. 24: Nothing worthwhile is achieved on the first attempt. You have to keep chipping away. Think of a diamond — in its rough form it is a very boring lump of rock.

Help from others

If you are feeling overwhelmed by a task, don't be afraid to ask for help. This can move you quickly from procrastination mode to proactive mode.

Sometimes a task is just too big for one person, but your superiors haven't recognised this. Have you told them? Sit down and make a list of all the tasks you have to do in the given time frame. Or, keep a time log for a day or two, so you can show them what you're *really* doing. Until you know clearly what you are being asked to do, how can you explain the challenges to anyone else? When you clearly understand what is being asked of you, and have some solutions to suggest, ask your team leader for help.

Don't be a martyr. If you can't do something, be prepared to say so. It is human nature to keep delegating until something or someone cries halt. Our children do it, our spouses do it — why should employers be different? Without meaning to be unfair, most bosses will continue to load a willing horse.

Perhaps you've offered to help someone else. Sometimes the people around you are better at delegating, upwards or downwards, than you are, but if you procrastinate on the tasks you've accepted, you and the people around you are going to be very frustrated.

Dealing with other people

Be tactful and considerate of the opinions of others, but don't let their views keep you from completing your tasks. Treat everyone fairly. Come to terms with potential adversaries. Some of your worries may be unfounded, but if there is conflict try to sort it out before work starts. If you cannot get resolution, you'll just have to keep working regardless. Keep attention focused on the task, not the person. If you let your feelings about them become a reason for you to procrastinate, other people are controlling your life. Anxiety will be the result.

Humour
Humour is a wonderful confidence booster and has a very therapeutic effect. When all else fails, laugh about it.

One area at a time
Remember, don't try to change everything that you're unhappy with in one go. (You'll blow yourself out of the water.) It is a certain guarantee for failure. Choose one area where procrastination is hurting you. Make a firm decision to deal with it, make a plan, set a deadline, tell someone who will support you, plan your rewards, and *get started*.

No excuses!

Chapter 12

Creative procrastination — learning what to go slow on

HOW TO ENJOY LIFE AND STILL ACHIEVE

I love explaining creative procrastination. It's like telling people that sometimes chocolate and ice-cream are actually good for you! You thought procrastination was a naughty word, didn't you? You're only partly right.

That bogey — negative procrastination — is bad. It occurs when we allow trivia to block us from having a fulfilled, happy and productive life. On the other hand, creative procrastination is good. It is deliberate — planning and scheduling time for your own use. It is also choosing to procrastinate on the flag-waving Reactive activities, so that you can work on long-term Proactive activities.

As we discussed in the previous chapter, negative procrastination is putting off until tomorrow that which should be done today.

My definition of creative procrastination is: *putting off until tomorrow things that won't advance your life plan by being done today.* It is also the planned and deliberate gift of prime time to yourself, regularly, to do what gives you greatest satisfaction — including doing nothing, if that is your choice. It is learning how to leave undone those things which didn't really need to be done, so that you achieve balance and satisfaction in your life.

Many of us have been brought up to regard 'doing nothing' as bad. Is it? How about adopting a new paradigm about 'think time' and 'play time'? The following comment illustrates this way of thinking:

> Sometimes we simply need to unlearn our polarized belief that only work is important and realize that without refreshing, renewing play, we lower our capacity for high-quality work and our ability to enjoy life fully. (McGee-Cooper and Trammell, 1994)

To achieve true management of our time, we must pay attention to health, relaxation and creativity, stress reduction, and sheer joy of living — which means having fun!

Super-efficiency is *not* necessarily what time management is about, in my opinion, despite what we've been taught in the past. In some business quarters, thank goodness, we are starting to get some common sense about balance in life, and less emphasis on commercialism, urgency, frenetic energy, making a quick buck, and feeling that we can't ease up for a minute or we might miss an opportunity to further ourselves. Things are starting to change.

WHAT TO PROCRASTINATE ON

How does the 80/20 rule apply in creative procrastination? Learn to focus on the activities that make a difference. Whatever you focus on you will be good at. Focus on negative influences in your life and you will be excellently negative; focus on 'busy work' and you will be excellent on detail and trivia; focus on the major task or tasks that are going to propel you to new levels of achievement and you will reach those new levels and beyond. As you focus on excluding or procrastinating on the things which do not matter and spend time on meaningful projects and people, over time you dramatically improve your quality of life.

It does take practice to be comfortable with this balance, but if you keep focusing on the top priority activities in each day, and keep focused on your long-term goals as well as your values, one day, I promise you, you'll suddenly realise that the trivia is simply not taking as much of your time.

CONCENTRATION

Concentration is really where all our study on time management takes us. If you have the ability to concentrate 100 percent on a significant task until it is finished, without distraction or diversion, or can very quickly refocus back again if you are distracted, you cannot help but succeed with that task. Concentration, or persistence, is self-discipline in action. That concentration means that you have creatively procrastinated on other activities. You have shut them out.

'DO WHAT YOU LOVE, THE MONEY WILL FOLLOW . . . '

For many people, work is creative: they love what they do, and feel fulfilled in doing it. Mark Twain said, 'The secret of success is making your vocation your vacation'. Marsha Sinetar, in her book *Do What you Love, the Money will Follow* (1987), says:

> . . . work is a way of being. A balanced person is always moving toward full participation in life, and growing in self-awareness, trust and high self-esteem. Abraham Maslow calls such healthy personalities 'self-actualizing' which means growing whole. They have taken moment-to-moment risks to ensure that their entire lives become an

outward expression of their true inner selves. They have a sense of their own worth and are likely to experiment, to be creative, to ask for what they want and need. Their high self-esteem and subsequent risk-taking/creativity brings them skills that help them find the work they want, and to stick to their choices until financial rewards come. Work is a way of being, an expression of love. It is also often a slow and difficult path of self-discipline, perseverance and integrity.

Others may not be passionate about their daily work, but they put time into other pursuits which fulfil and energise them. They take classes, do volunteer work, polish their skills in sport or hobbies, build a part-time business or a network marketing business in their discretionary time, or any of a multitude of other activities. In years to come, opportunities may arise for these people to turn the things they enjoy doing into their vocation.

HOWEVER, WE NEED TIME OUT

Even if we fall into the work-loving category (and I do) we still have to remind ourselves to take 'unwind' time. If I hadn't done crazy things like get up in the pre-dawn hours, taken my laptop on holiday, and set aside many weekend hours to work, I wouldn't have finished this book. I had a strong and worthwhile goal that created momentum, and so giving up some of my sleep and recreational hours never seemed a hardship. To balance the long hours, however, I planned regular times for my close relationships, during which those special people had my undivided attention. I also planned sleep-in times, light-reading times, and holidays without a computer or non-fiction book in sight. Last Christmas, for instance, I decided that work stopped on Christmas Eve. As well as enjoying family activities, I went cruising on a yacht for five days with four girlfriends, and while they fished I read novels voraciously. Because I had given myself permission to do nothing that looked like work for two weeks, there was not one skerrick of guilt about not working on my book (even though I knew that a deadline was looming!).

Many people have to work hard in the short term — for example, those establishing a business — and so for a time their lives are out of balance. The key factor is that no matter what the reason, those of us who happily work long hours have to remind ourselves constantly not to run the schedule indefinitely. Otherwise we are in danger of becoming workaholics with broken health and relationships.

BEWARE OF HURRY SICKNESS

Hurry sickness is a new medical term. Dr Larry Dossey (1984) says it is 'expressed as heart disease, high blood pressure, or depression of our immune function, leading to an increased susceptibility to infection and cancer'.

The Japanese have a word, *karoshi*, for death by overwork. I'm sure the same condition is found in other countries also; in Japan widows are suing their husbands' employers.

Now that more women are moving into senior executive positions and running their own businesses, their rate of stress-related sickness such as strokes and heart attacks is increasing to match that of the men. I know we want equality, but of this sort?

If you're not careful, you'll find you are so busy being busy that you are ruled by time instead of controlling it to your long-term benefit. The average businessperson spends most of the day responding to the external demands of colleagues, customers, and suppliers. Many feel guilty if they stop to engage in future planning or are seen to be sitting still. The fact that free-form thinking is going on seems not to count, because they've been taught it is wrong to be idle. This kind of person doesn't feel comfortable using discretionary time as they choose until everyone else's needs and demands have been satisfied, and when nothing obvious is waiting to be done (which is virtually never).

LISTEN TO YOUR BODY

It is common to ignore the messages our bodies are trying to give us and keep working even when ill or exhausted, because we are so conditioned to using our time 'fully'. I've ignored those messages myself, but guess what — I never win an argument with my body! Pushing yourself in this way simply leads to stress, illness and inefficiency.

The owner of a day-care centre had just had a staff member leave, causing her to have to work longer shifts each day. She was so tired that she couldn't even see that 'more hours' did not equal 'more productivity'. She was starting her days feeling tired; pushing herself to do everything she thought she 'ought' to be doing and not delegating tasks to others because she didn't want to be 'unfair'. Each day she got less and less done, and felt more and more exhausted. She wondered why she had a cold, and felt guilty about all manner of things that weren't flowing well. I sent her home for a sleep and advised her to find someone to take over so she could have the next day off. From this experience she learned that sometimes maximum efficiency comes from giving yourself permission to stop.

Don't feel guilty about stopping when you're tired.

WHAT ARE WE WORKING FOR?

There are still many corporate cultures that encourage their employees to be 'married' to the job, and there are an increasing number of self-employed people who work well in excess of 60–70 hours per week. There is also another type of person who knows no other way than to work extraordinarily long hours. Their sense of identity is anchored in their work. They are actually out of balance — work-centred, instead of fully integrated and grounded people who have a strong sense of personal identity.

It is possible to work long hours and still have balance in your life. Successful people are very productive people, and none that I know have got there by working only 40 hours a week. Balance for such people, however, has to be planned for and scheduled in, or it tends to slide unprotestingly away.

I believe that part of the problem lies in the good old work ethic many of us had instilled from a young age. I absolutely agree that when we're working we should work hard and fast. That's the mark of a winner. Let's consider, though, why *do* we work?

Mostly it's so we can live. What does 'to live' mean for you? Is it to provide sufficient money for food, health, a roof over your head, to pay the bills, have a little spare for some of the nice things of life, and a comfortable retirement? It may also include contributing to society in whatever way is important to you.

Some people have a powerful drive to rise to the top of their profession, with all the monetary advantages that suggests. Others may want to spend time travelling in other countries. Yet others may be totally fulfilled by living a very quiet life, surrounded by family and friends and working in the same profession all their lives. Everyone will have different variations on the same theme. At the end of the day, most of us would like to say we work to live, rather than live to work, but for some there will be an uncomfortable little internal niggle that they are not really speaking the truth.

WHAT ABOUT 'QUALITY OF LIFE'?

It's sad to hear someone say: 'My life has been wasted.' How awful to be coming to the end of your life and feel that you hadn't reached your potential. Some of these unfortunate people may have been negative procrastinators or perhaps they've filled their lives with trivia. It probably also means that they haven't included satisfying and fulfilling activities in their regular schedule. Often the extra amount of time spent doing something memorable is not very much or, when looking back, you realise that what you didn't do, because you were out having fun, didn't matter anyway.

How often have you heard people say, 'When I've got visitors I see local places I would otherwise ignore.' Some years ago I lived at Ninety Mile Beach, in the Far North of New Zealand. My home was very close to the water, and sure enough, I found that after about six months I started to take it for granted. Fortunately for my memory bank, in the last year I made a new friend. Rose, who lived in the nearby town, loved the beach with a passion. Why she hadn't bought at the beach I'll never know, because every possible weekend she would jump into her car and come out. Often she would turn up at my place and say, 'Come on Robyn, let's go down to the beach.' I would be engrossed in 'absolutely exciting' projects like housework, ironing or gardening, and have to make a conscious effort to shift my focus to recreation. The funny thing is — I don't remember the uncompleted housework ever being a major problem. The necessary stuff somehow always got done. But I do remember having many wonderful summer days on the beach with Rose.

HOW TO FIND TIME TO PLAY AND TO THINK

If you plan your recreational time as carefully as you do your business activities, it is surprising how many special and memorable events can be fitted in to your life. Sometimes people look at me in horror when I suggest that they set aside special time for their partners and families. One or two have said that their partners become quite irate at being treated as a 'scheduled item'. In reply, I ask them to consider how much they remember of the last month's unscheduled 'go with the flow' activities with their loved ones. Are there any enriching highlights that jump out at them from last week's TV viewing with their partner? I then ask them to think about the last time they arranged a special outing. How much detail comes to mind? Who did they see? What was the day like? What did they eat, and where? In this area, as with everything else in the way we use our lives, planning is the key. It isn't restrictive — it's liberating and enriching. It actually allows more flexibility.

This idea of scheduling in your family and recreational activities may seem very alien. You may have to make quite major lifestyle changes. Learn to be analytical about your work habits, your achievements, and your long-term plans. Don't be one-eyed. Learn to think outside of the square boxes of your brain — to become a lateral thinker. Look for ways to delegate less important work to others and to arrange your business so that you are not the only person with your interests at heart. Find ways to 'duplicate' yourself.

One of my clients has a large and rapidly increasing business. When he first came to see me, he explained that he doesn't really enjoy being on the workshop site, or in the office. He feels more productive when he's at a distance, letting other people do the hands-on, day-to-day work. His skill is in thinking up new ideas, roving around spotting new opportunities, and spending time learning new things to help implement future developments. Although his staff don't see him very often, he is very aware of the profit and loss position of the company, and has his finger very much on the performance of each employee. He is also a very effective delegator, and has chosen his staff well.

Because many of his employees are more conventional thinkers, he was concerned that perhaps he was off-beam with this approach. I believe that he is more on track than most of the people I know. I also believe that we are going to see more and more people working towards this style of management. This man has got a handle on creative procrastination!

MUST GO - IT'S TIME FOR MY CORONARY!

UNDERSTAND WHAT DRIVES YOU

We often keep our noses to the grindstone, doing the work in front of us, and getting the pay-rises offered (if we're lucky), without really regarding what we want out of life. Again I want to stress — what are your values? Are they congruent with your goals? What are you wanting to achieve, not just today, not just this week, but further out into the future? By taking time to listen to your inner self, and working on the exercises at the beginning of the book, you will eventually get clear on what *really* matters to you. Without that clarity, you just can't achieve real peace of mind. Remember, life management, not just time management.

One of my clients discussed this values/goals issue with me, over a six-week period. It is often one of the hardest issues for people to get a clear grip on. She is a hardworking wife and mother, and was at that time a salesperson. All her life she has been efficient — the sort who unintentionally makes a less-organised person feel inferior, simply because she seems to pack a huge amount of activity into every day. Her passion, however, is for the theatre.

Through conversations with me, she realised that her values — which revolved primarily round her wife, mother, theatre, and community service roles — didn't fit with her financial and work goals. Although her income was useful to the family budget, it was possible for them to manage with less, if necessary. Also, her awesome amount of activity didn't actually make her feel fulfilled as a person. We talked about lateral thinking regarding her income creation. However, it was only when she gave herself enough time to sit back and really analyse her life that, like a bolt from the sky, she suddenly saw what to do. By changing her work direction, and carving a specialist niche in the drama field, she could bring her values and her goals into congruence, and achieve personal satisfaction.

She could have kept on doing a good job in her sales role, and her bosses were certainly very happy with her results. However, the lack of congruence between, on one hand, her work and financial goals, and on the other, her values, was making her an increasingly dissatisfied person. Because she had such a happy home life she couldn't understand what was wrong. It seemed so ungrateful to be dissatisfied! By looking more closely at her core values, talking to me and others, and expanding her thinking with reading and learning, she opened her mind to other possibilities. Now, a few years later, she has her own drama school for young children. For a while she'll probably make less money, but in fact that was never the issue. She is happy, fulfilled, following her dream, and making a difference in the lives of many youngsters.

THE CHOICES ARE YOURS — FLEXIBILITY

I used to think that if I worked hard and reached certain achievements I would *then* be able to reward myself. Of course that still applies. There is a huge power in delayed gratification. However, when we start to think laterally about incorporating elements of long-term goals into our 'now' time, it is surprising what opportunities arise. You may wish to travel extensively overseas, and not be able to afford a long trip just now. What stops you from having a week or two of your annual leave in another country? Often it costs virtually no more than to travel internally. Our minds, rather than the reality of the situation, are the biggest blocks to exciting living and new possibilities.

We hear people talk about stopping to smell the flowers. How often do you *really* look around you? When did you last go for a walk, or a run, in some beautiful natural setting? Have you been looking for the latest change of the seasons? When did you last sit and look at the sea for more than two minutes? When did you last stop your busy-ness and just observe the world around you?

No-one can be totally active every minute of every day. Grant yourself permission to balance your day according to your values, needs, and moods. It is your responsibility — no-one else's — to make these choices. You cannot blame anyone else for lack of time — you are the person in charge of yourself.

Many of us feel guilty if we are not 'doing work' every minute of a working day. I remember getting a fresh perspective on this when I first met my husband. I had been recommended to ring him to find out about buying a new home. When we were setting the appointment, he said, 'I've got a game of squash this afternoon, but I'll be free by three o'clock. Have the kettle on, and I'll have a cup of tea with you while we discuss houses.'

I remember thinking, 'Wow! This guy does business in a different way.' I didn't appreciate at that point that he did a lot of evening and weekend work, when the rest of the world had stopped for the day, or the week — but even so, his attitude was refreshing. What it said to me was that the way he did business included giving himself time for recreation in the day, and that was okay.

I had been so conditioned to perform in a certain way that I wouldn't have dreamed of going off to do something for myself (on a regular basis) in the middle of the afternoon. And even if I had arranged to make up for it by working late, there is no way I would have told a client, in case they thought I was being a slacker. The funny thing was — I realised I had no problem with someone else doing it. My perceptions had a lot to do with self-esteem — I would have felt irresponsible and unworthy of my pay, even though every boss I had ever worked for had always had 110 percent of my commitment. The interesting thing is that if you make a decision to take some time for yourself, ensure that no-one is being disadvantaged by your absence, and go and do it — the world does not stop! Flexibility is okay!

GIVE SOMEONE PERMISSION TO INTERRUPT YOU

Remember the theory that work expands to fit the time available? Learn to contract the time you give to a task. How? Usually, I would say that it is a good habit to allow more time to complete a task than you think you need, as this allows for unexpected interruptions. It doesn't always work, however. We need to put our 'laser beam' of concentration on our activities and ask: Is this activity vital to my long-term future or is it only busy work?

If you have a problem taking too long on a task, deliberately set yourself up so that someone will interrupt you at a specified time. Box yourself in — this forces you to stop what you are doing. Discuss the issue with a good friend or family member who has a vested interest in getting you to spend some quality time with them. It is quite hard to change your old behaviour patterns on your own. Give them permission to hang a guilt trip on you! This is constructive guilt — not the negative sort described next.

GUILT

We mentioned this briefly when discussing flexibility. The negative form of guilt is a close bedfellow of the lack of self-esteem that sometimes prevents us from taking time for ourselves. Do you sometimes feel unworthy of a treat that involves giving yourself some time out because you think you don't 'deserve' a reward? People who don't manage their time very well often have these feelings. A couple of tips to overcome them are:

1. Learn how to overcome procrastination (see the previous chapter).
2. Make a regular affirmation such as: 'I deserve fun. I regularly make time for fun.'

If you are getting stale on a project, take a short break, but don't feel guilty about needing that break. Be clear in your mind that the break is going to enable you to return to the task thinking more clearly and more effectively. You have two choices: to feel good about the break, or guilty. Since rest is essential, learn to enjoy it.

CREATE AWARENESS OF INDIVIDUAL RHYTHMS

- When do you feel really sharp?
- Do your feet hit the floor gladly first thing, or is it 'Oh no, kill that alarm clock'?

- Do you drag off to bed around 9.30–10 pm or earlier, or are you a night owl?
- When is your best creative time? Have you ever noticed? Morning? Afternoon? Middle of the night?
- How do your family and colleagues perceive you in this respect?
- What is your optimum environment for productivity?
- How do you feel you work best? In quiet? With noise and buzz? Lots of people around?

We all have different rhythms and different learning styles. Learn yours. For instance, are you an owl or a fowl — a night person or early morning ray of sunshine? Do you find it easier to work with or without music playing? What sort of music? We are all more effective if we work within our rhythms rather than in spite of them: if you like, creatively procrastinating until we have some chance of success. Don't, however, use that as an excuse for never getting started!

WORK WITH YOUR PERSONAL STYLE, NOT AGAINST IT

Don't make important decisions or have important meetings in your slower times. Instead, do routine things such as phone calls, paperwork, and so on. If you're tired, or not feeling particularly positive don't, for example, try ringing new prospects or making important calls. Get to know your rhythms.

Recognise your style. If you are left-brain focused you will like things to be orderly and systematic. You'll like lists, details, and things put back in their place.

Right-brain people like to talk things over, won't mind a bit of chaos, or things spread around. If they've got a 'visually inviting' environment they'll work more effectively.

Be aware, also, of the styles of the people who work with you. I remember one workplace where the boss and I must have been operating from different polarities. To him the most important thing was having two staff members sitting in the attractive front offices so that any walk-in customers could be referred to them quickly by the receptionist. To my boss's mind, that was effective. It nearly drove me insane. One week I was moved every day, and on one particular day I was moved three times. I like to have all my files and tools (stapler, envelopes, forms, and so on) at my fingertips. I can then operate at maximum efficiency because I don't have to go on a hunt every time I address an envelope, or need a rubber or a paper-clip. I regularly do two things at once — concurrent activity — such as filling in paperwork while I wait for someone to answer the phone. It's not possible to be that organised if you're always moving. In fact, every time I shift desks my natural instinct is to 'nest-build' — to have everything in place around me before I can start to work. By the time I got to lunchtime and I'd ended up at the third desk, I'd also ended up on the verge of tears!

The same office was quite noisy, with a radio playing loudly all the time and the staff calling out to each other from room to room. At first it looked like a fun place to be, but within a few months it made working from my serene, peaceful home seem like heaven. Not surprisingly, I only lasted six months.

The benefit of understanding your own personality is that you can use this knowledge to enjoy life more, as well as be more effective.

Exercise 6

Ask yourself:

- How many hours a week do I work? (Honestly!)
- Am I happy with that, or would I prefer to work less? Or more?
- What drives me?
- Do I have enough fun time?

- Do I have enough regular 'relax' time with my family and friends?
- Which of the tasks that I'm presently doing could I delegate?
- How often do I have to push my weary body, when every muscle and fibre screams 'Stop'?
- Thinking laterally, what can I do about it?
- When did I last stop to think, and write, about the 'big' issues of life — how I want my life to be, whether my activities are congruent with my values, and so on?
- When did I last take an hour (or more) to forward plan?
- How often do I do forward planning?
- When I last took some planning time, how did I feel?
- Do I feel I have regular enough think times?
- What fun activities am I currently telling myself I haven't got time to do?
- Am I sure about that? (Spend some time thinking laterally about other ways of looking at it. Don't stop until you've come up with at least three alternatives.)
- Who has an interest in helping me get a better life balance?
- When am I most productive?
- What is my personality style? Do I like order and structure, or happy chaos? Quiet, or lots of noise and action going on around me?
- How do the people around me like to work?

Write down your own personal affirmations about quality of life.

A FINAL THOUGHT

Deliberately choose to set aside some time in every day to do something for yourself. Who wants to spend most of their day in reactive mode, doing the things that everyone else wants them to do?

KEY POINT No. 25: Life is for living — take time to enjoy it.

Chapter 13

Surviving the never-ending flow of paper

This subject I find fascinating, probably because I have an on-going love affair with paper. I used to be your traditional hoarder. Over the years I've slowly, one step at a time, learnt to control my magpie tendencies, but believe me, those of you who struggle with letting go of paper (for whatever reasons) I do understand! Here are some key tips to give you control over this ever-flowing river of processed trees!

Those of you who identify with my admission will like the comment made by one of my 'Win the Paper War' course participants. She had listened with a growing sense of relief as the other members of the group explained why they were there and what their individual challenges were.

'Oh,' she said, 'we're like alcoholics, but it's paper we're addicted to. Robyn, you should start a group called Paperholics Anonymous!' A roar of laughter went round the room. They all knew exactly what she meant!

OUR CONVERSATIONS ABOUT MESSY DESKS!

Are you one of those people who justifies a messy desk?

'I know exactly where everything is!' they say as they look at the town tip spread out on their desk. Yes, they might — but how much time do they spend rifling through to find the urgent report that has to be reviewed before the meeting in ten minutes! And what about the bank account that needs reconciling? They had 'just put it somewhere here'. It's now three weeks later, and they spend ten minutes looking for it before they can balance the cheque-book. It's urgent now — if it doesn't balance the bank might bounce the next cheque right back!

How much time do you spend weekly in searching for mislaid paper?

What is *your* desk like?

If someone who doesn't know you walked into your office right now, what sort of person would they think you are? Messy people are less likely to be considered for promotion, and less likely to be given new opportunities, because they're seen as not managing their current load very well.

A cluttered desk indicates a cluttered mind. Why do you let it get cluttered? Is it because you think that putting an important item on the desk rather than in a file means you won't forget it?

WELL, THOSE ARE THE ESSENTIALS —
NOW, WHAT DO WE DO WITH THE REST?

Does that work? Be warned. Keeping track of where things *might* be takes lots of mental energy. Trying to ignore the mess takes even more.

Let's start at the beginning. When you next front up to your desk, take everything off it, pile the 'stuff' either on the chair or the floor, wipe the desk down, and then put back only the essentials. Notice how you feel when it's all clean and tidy.

Okay, that's a taste of freedom — now, what do you do with the debris? Here are some practical steps to eliminating debris and enjoying that freedom every day.

SETTING UP THE OFFICE
The fittings
Obvious as the need for filing equipment and good storage seems, I have seen many people trying their hardest to be organised, but with nowhere to actually put things.

The most vital need for anyone serious about a smoothly functioning workspace is the right equipment. For anyone with paperwork to handle, it is impossible to be efficient unless you have some sort of shelving, a filing cabinet or box of some kind, and a desk of some sort — preferably with at least three drawers, or a top drawer and a file drawer.

The space closest to where you sit is your most valuable — guard it like precious jewels. Make sure that the things you use constantly are close enough for you to reach without having to stand up, or stretch very far. And don't let space-stealers with low value sneak in!

Position your desk so you don't have to eyeball passers-by. If necesssary, position a tall plant where it creates a visual barrier.

Make sure your chair is not only comfortable, but also ergonomically correct. Who needs a bad back caused by beavering away over a desk or computer for hours.

While we're talking about the physical features of your office, spare a thought for the colour. Green, blue-green and blue will help you concentrate. Peach and pink help your creativity.

Desks

Everyone, from senior executives to homemakers and students, functions better if they have a desk of their own, with drawers. I've known people who work with only a drawerless table. Of course you can manage, but it means you have to create alternative storage systems.

Filing equipment

Filing cabinets come in many styles. There are desks with a filing drawer fitted. These are fine for many workers. There are two-, three-, or four-drawer cabinets. They are excellent if space is not at a premium and usually only one person at a time needs to use them. There are cardboard or wooden filing boxes, which are modelled on the drawer system. These can be kept in a cupboard, or under your desk, and work well for one person's filing or for someone working a small business from home. And there are upright shelf file systems. Although more expensive, this is the most efficient method for larger, more complex organisations. More than one person can access them at a time, they work on a colour-code filing system which makes misfiling significantly harder to do, and they take up less space in the room. However, their coding system is more complex and takes longer to set up, as you need to refer to an index while coding.

CLEANING UP THE EXISTING MESS! HOW TO BECOME A 'KAOS' BUSTER

I'm going to be very assumptive and presume that at least some of my readers are in a state of chaos: that their office or desk would currently give a graffiti tagger ideas. Those of you who are already perfect in this area will probably have some friend or associate who needs to have this chapter pointed out to them!

Because I enjoy cleaning out cupboards and creating workable systems (yes, I know that's weird!), I thought everyone knew how to do the following steps. I finally realised a few years ago that I was very wrong. The very idea of initiating a sort-out is enough to send some poor folk into a tail-spin, mainly because they don't know how to start. The whole task seems just too overwhelming!

The good news is that everyone I've worked with to conquer their chaos has been able to sustain order once it was in place, and some who had the worst mess have even gone on to help other people. The key is breaking the task down into small, simple steps, and if necessary getting a friend to help you.

Necessary equipment

1. As discussed above: a desk, shelves and the appropriate filing system for your needs.
2. Plenty of drop files, label holders and labels if working with traditional filing systems. If you choose one of the modern upright systems the company who sells it to you will provide the necessary 'software'.
3. A bundle of manilla folders (get the coloured ones if you like pretty things around you).
4. Make sure you have plenty of rubbish sacks!
5. Have some cardboard document boxes for storage of semi-archival material, such as accounts and correspondence of previous years.
6. Get a bundle of periodicals boxes. (Ask at your friendly stationers — document and periodical boxes come folded flat.) If you're not sure what periodical boxes are, go into your nearest library and see how they store pamphlets, magazines

and other more ephemeral material. The beauty of these little treasures is that you can store skinny, small items and loose pieces of paper upright. By using some of your brightly coloured manilla folders you can also create sub-categories within your pamphlet boxes.

The reason for these storage boxes? As soon as you stack material in a heap you are asking for lost paper and a future mess. You can't label a heap, it will never be put back in the same order, and it has no solid shape for you to easily control. At best it can only perch on a desk, a shelf, or in a cupboard.

A basic rule of storage is: where possible store things upright, even document boxes and books. As soon as you have to shift something off a heap to get at an item further down, you are inviting trouble as other things are sure to be misplaced in the process. Another vital rule is to label everything clearly. If you change the contents you can always put a new sticker on the box. If you're reluctant to label something in case you have to relabel it, write in pencil.

Necessary attitude
Be prepared to have fun and enjoy the task in hand. You're going to feel great when it's done.

Goal
Your goal is to eliminate the mess from your work station, and to give you a feeling of power and control over your environment and your work. You will achieve this by having only one place for each item or category, setting up effective storage systems, and developing a method of keeping work off the desk until you are ready to do it.

Plan of attack

1. Set aside as much time as you need to complete the task. Depending on the quantity of paper, you may need anything from an hour or two to a whole day.

2. Go through every cupboard, file, drawer and desk. Take everything out. Pile it all on the floor. Handle each piece of paper. Throw out any obviously obsolete material. With the rest, identify the topic, and sort into broad categories, e.g.: Bank Statements; Property; Tax; Memos; Meeting Agendas; Current Action; Long-term Action; Future Ideas; Staff.

   For every new category, create a pile. As you create each one, write the topic on a piece of paper and place it so it protrudes from the pile. You can then identify at a glance (while you're still sorting) what the heaps are. Also make heaps of stationery, envelopes, stamps, pens, and any other miscellaneous items.

3. Systematically work through your entire office. You must not begin to sort out the separate piles until every item has been placed in a labelled pile.

4. Be ruthless with the rubbish. Constantly ask yourself:
   - Do I need this?
   - When was the last time I looked at it?
   - What is the worst thing that will happen if I don't have it?
   - Does anyone else have another copy?

   There'll almost always be a worse magpie than you whom you can rely on to be the company hoarder! Or there may be a designated back-up system, and you're just duplicating it.

5. Don't be side-tracked into reading all the old stuff at this point. You are only sorting it, not making final decisions. If you want to closely examine something before deciding its fate, make a heap of To Read Later or To Do. If you find those two heaps have 90 percent of your paper, you're not

being tough enough on yourself and may need some help.

6. Work quickly. If you're not very self-disciplined, you may need to get someone to stand over you so that you do. I've taken this 'stand-over' role when working with quite a few people. Each of them commented that, if they hadn't had me there, they would have maintained momentum for about fifteen minutes and then been distracted into some interesting little by-way. The allotted time would have gone, and they would have been in a worse mess. It's more fun with someone else, too, if tidying up isn't your favourite activity.

7. Check that every drawer, shelf and cupboard is completely empty. Now, and only now, are you allowed to start putting things back. If you start sooner, you'll end up putting useful things on top of old junk, just perpetuating the clutter and never clearing your head. Have you ever inherited someone else's office, left their junk in the cupboards and drawers in case it was important, never looked at it again, and a year later wondered why you haven't got much room?

8. A lot of material has already gone into the rubbish sacks, but now you are going to fine-tune each heap as you place it in its final home. Keeping uppermost in your mind the questions in step 4, handle each item. Again, remember, you are not thoroughly reading everything — you're just skimming to check that you (a) need to keep this item, and (b) you're putting it in the right place. Be ruthless.

9. Rearrange books, alphabetically by author or by subject (unless you've only got a handful). Return those that have 'accidently' forgotten to return to their rightful owners (there speaks an ex-librarian!).

10. If it's paper to go in the filing cabinet, think: 'What would I be likely to look for this under, in a month's time?' If it's equipment, think: 'How often do I use this, and where is it

going to be most useful?' If it's something you're using all the time, like a stapler or a container of paper-clips, you'll probably have it in the top drawer of your desk. Never have regularly used items more than an arm's-reach away.

11. As you place material in files, *label* each file. If you think you might forget your chosen headings, label the individual material as well.

I encourage people to have as little clutter as possible on top of their desks. Have you ever felt that there isn't much space on your desk to work? It may be the work waiting to grab you round the throat, and we'll deal with that soon. Or is it because the ruler, rubber, stapler, paper-punch, paper-clips, and other miscellaneous equipment are taking up 50 percent of your desk-top?

One caution — the way you set up your desk and office partly relies on the type of mind you have. Left-brain, organised people like their things systematic, convenient, logically placed, and probably out of sight; right-brain, creative folk like the stimulation of brightly coloured things around them, visual, in sight. Both are right — mess is not!

We're finished being Kaos Busters, but we have to know how to handle new material as it deluges us.

HOW WE CONCENTRATE — A CRITICAL FACT YOU NEED TO KNOW

Before we continue with the next stage, how to set up your desk, I think it's time to give you a very important piece of information about the way we concentrate. When working manually with paper of any sort, the attention span of most people is about twenty minutes. It goes in a wave pattern. At the beginning of the task we can concentrate fully, and are unlikely to interrupt ourselves. However, as the minutes tick by the chance of self-interruptions increases. If you have multitudes of cute little distractions waving hands at you in the form of all those other pieces of paper on your desk, it becomes increasingly difficult to maintain total focus on what you are doing. Suddenly you'll find yourself with the phone in your hand, some other paper has jumped in under your nose, or you're half-way down the hall to check on the details of another job. This is why every time management specialist will say: 'Keep your desk clear of all but what you're working on.' By doing so you are hugely reducing the chance of temptation.

Working with computers is the exception to the rule. I think it's something to do with the way we interact with computers. Our mind, our eyes, and our hands are engaged, and the screen constantly changes. Everyone agrees that we have a much greater attention span when working with a keyboard and screen.

KEEPING THE PAPER FLOWING, ONCE WE'RE ORGANISED

I strongly recommend the following system for your desk, if you have three drawers. If you have six, you can store spare stationery on one side. If you only have one drawer you need some stacker trays, preferably positioned slightly above your vision, or behind you but within reach. (I'll tell you why shortly.)

Drawer 1

Your top drawer is where you keep the tools you need all the time, e.g. stapler, paper-clips, ruler, rubber, etc. Throw out the chewing gum, old broken sunglasses, spare packs of staples for the stapler you lost two years ago, and the bus tickets you might use if your car breaks down. Remember, the space closest to you is precious.

Sometimes people say they'd rather keep their tools on top of their desk. You have to decide whether the fraction of a second it takes to open and reach into your neat and tidy top drawer justifies the free space you'll create and the extra working room you'll have on top of your desk. I believe it does, but as I mentioned above, you may prefer a visual display.

Drawer 2

Use this for your current work, which used to decorate the top of your desk. It's close, it's comfortable to reach into (you don't have to bend to look in it), and if you're constantly getting things from it you don't forget what's in there.

Some people keep their current work in manilla folders. Others use clear plastic two-sided pouches or envelopes, because you can see what's in them and items are less likely to fall out. And yet others, especially when first getting into the discipline of moving work off the desk, are afraid of losing sight of items in the folders, and feel more comfortable with all work loose in the drawer. (I encourage you to train yourself to use folders or plastic pouches as quickly as possible — they are actually more controllable.)

I suggest no more than three files in this drawer:
- current action
- long-term projects.
  These could be kept in the filing cabinet, but you may feel happier having them where you constantly see them.
- reading file (if it doesn't get too thick).

If you have too many choices of filing places it can be very embarrassing if you have to find something quickly. Believe me, I've tried it. Imagine keeping a caller on hold while you furiously thumb through six different files, trying to sound efficient when really you can't remember whether that vital piece of paper is in Current Action, Meetings, Phone Calls, or some other category you thought was a good idea when you set up your glorious new system!

Drawer 3

This is your dump drawer. Here place the trivial paper that does-n't justify filing, but which you're not ready to throw out just yet. I call it my 'half-way to File 13 (rubbish bin)' drawer. I have things such as flyers about courses I've enrolled for and may need to check some detail on, newsletters that will be superfluous in a short while and don't justify filing, printing jobs that have been proofed and sent to the printer, and so on. It makes a great safety net. Occasionally you'll have reason to look for something in that drawer. When you do, throw out anything that's obviously obso-lete. You'll find the drawer never fills up.

IN- AND OUT-TRAYS — TRAPS FOR THE UNWARY!

We'd better talk about in- and out-trays here. Many people have them in pride of place on their desks, breeding prodigiously.

First of all, why do you need an out-tray? If you're scrupulous about keeping it empty, good on you. Most people have all kinds of treasures languishing there.

Here's a little trick to make out-trays obsolete, which I learnt from being a busy mother. As I worked in one room, anything which belonged elsewhere was put near the door so that I could take it with me the next time I went in that direction. Many business people use a similar system. (All the best ideas are really simple!) If you are working on the philosophy of keeping only your current task on your desk, you want to remove the task as soon as it's completed. Even an out-tray is still a visual distraction.

As I finish with any item, I place it on the floor beside my chair. Which side of the chair depends on which part of the room it is to go to. The next time I stand up, I put whatever is on the floor in its parking place. This includes filing paper in the cabinet.

There are many benefits. There is never any filing waiting for a 'spare' moment; everything is put away while it is still fresh in your mind, which saves time refamiliarising yourself later; your office is always tidy (except for the small amount of paper on the floor around your chair if you haven't stood up for half-an-hour); and of course you're not distracting yourself.

If you must have an in-tray I believe it needs to be either above your line of vision, or behind you. Do be careful, though, the temptation is for all manner of miscellaneous items to snuggle in there. (Some people could have a nest of mice and they wouldn't know if the mice kept quiet — they never get to the bottom!)

If you are using your drawer system effectively, current work can be kept out of sight until you're ready to deal with it at the appointed time. If you've only got a small work area you may need to have mail and assorted in-coming material placed in an in-tray until you are ready to deal with it, but if you have another table or shelf, what about training yourself and others to park things there until you're ready to get to work on today's deluge? If others are in the habit of dumping on your desk, either train yourself to reposition their gifts, or train them!

THE TOP OF YOUR DESK

This is home for your diary, blotter, pen and pencil container, jotter pad for others if they take a call at your desk (you're using your diary, aren't you!), possibly a computer, and maybe a picture of your loved ones. Apart from that, you'll only have on the top of your desk what you're currently working on right now.

If a task requires a multitude of paper your desk may look cluttered while you're in the middle of the job. That's okay — paper from many tasks is not. If you are prioritising correctly, you won't be moving erratically from task to task — you'll be completing a job as far as possible before putting it to one side, at which point it would go back into the drawer. If you get interrupted, try to take the previous work to a logical stop point, and if necessary make a note of where you are up to before you deal with the interruption.

HELP! WHERE IS THAT PIECE OF PAPER?
In case you haven't yet got the message about little bits of paper — kill them! They are a major trap. Just ask a confirmed notemaker if they've ever lost a vital piece of paper. I promise you — they have. Do yourself a favour — write any notes in your diary. This is where a decent diary system comes into its own. If you've got two pages to a day, you have plenty of room to record phone numbers, key points of conversations, and any other information that would have formerly decorated scrappy bits of paper. Most seven-ring binder systems also have a monthly index system, so to find any vital piece of information is as easy as looking at your monthly index sheets (as long as you've indexed as you go). These same systems have facility to create project files, so any regular activity can have its own section in your diary. You virtually never lose information once you learn to use a diary effectively. Much better than rummaging through the rubbish bin!

KEY POINT No. 26: Out-of-control paper is like a stone thrown in a pool — the ripples affect those around.

CATCH A RAFT — HOW TO KEEP THE SYSTEMS RUNNING SMOOTHLY
We've got the systems sorted out, but now we have to keep them running smoothly. Maintaining this new efficiency is the vital issue. Are you going to maintain it? How? Let's look at specific techniques to help you.

We struggle daily with an ever-flowing river of paper. Relax, there are only four basic things you can do with any piece of paper. Catch a RAFT to keep you floating. If you don't, you'll drown.

- Read
- Act
- File
- Throw

Here are a few quick pointers for each function.

Read

1. Learn to skim read.
2. Don't read things you won't remember, and become aware of how much time you spend reading things which won't further you in any way (and which therefore belong in the Time-wasting Category).
3. Cancel magazines and papers you don't have time to read.
4. Create a reading file for the times you have to wait for someone or something. Never go anywhere without a back-up activity (even the fish and chip shop).
5. How many hours a month do you spend in the bathroom? Have a pile of useful reading material in there.
6. Go on a rapid reading course.
7. Read non-fiction books like you read newspapers. Most busy executives say they haven't time to keep up with the professional literature in their field, but they spend hundreds of hours reading newspapers. Even if you only skim one non-fiction book per week, and take away only the key points, you'll be way ahead of your opposition.
8. If it's your book, use a highlighter.
9. Plan regular reading times in your schedule.

Act

Figure K shows a breakdown of the Act function.

Act Now. As I mentioned in the section on time-wasters, try (where appropriate) to make a decision about each piece of paper

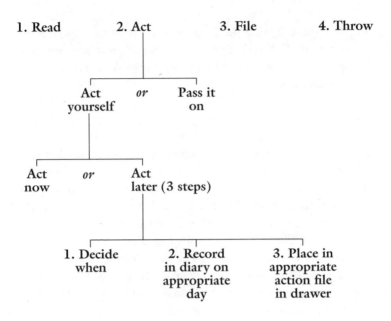

Figure K: The Act function

the first time you handle it. It saves warm-up time having to re-familiarise yourself with the issue, each time you pick it up.

Act later is the power point. To make it work for you, you must be using your diary or planner on a daily basis, or your paperwork will fall between the cracks of your good intentions!

The reason many people don't want to change the habit of keeping work on top of the desk is that they're scared they'll lose sight of important things if they are placed in a drawer, a filing cabinet, or a folder. Quite right, unless they're following these steps.

1. Make a realistic decision as to when you want to tackle the paperwork in your hand.
2. Record it in your planner, and make sure you refer to your planner daily.

3. Now you can safely put it out of sight. It won't emigrate, nor will it vanish. You don't have to worry about it again until the appropriate day. Instead you can work on today's priorities with an uncluttered mind.

File

Everything you keep costs you time and money. Around 85 percent of what we file is never looked at again, and yet many organisations spend huge amounts of money on storage, sometimes erecting special buildings. The emphasis needs to be on efficient retrieval, and keeping what may be needed for legal and business compliances, not just mindlessly storing paper.

Day-to-day filing in many companies seems to be a task that everyone tries to dodge. Why do we file things? Is it really a clerical function? I believe that in general the filing is best done by the person who generates the paper, and that includes the boss. Why? The person who works with the paper is in the best position to know where to put it when finished, and can do so rapidly because they're already familiar with the contents. Also, if you've put something away you'll be much more likely to remember where it is the next time you need it. Retrieval of information is, I believe, a management function because information is a valuable strategic resource. The harder it is to locate, the less valuable it is.

Here are some specific tips:

1. About every six months, have a purge of your filing cabinets. Appoint a day for the whole company to do the same task (and make sure you've got a rubbish collection the next day or a shredder organised!).

2. Make sure you have a labelling system that works for you. It could be alphabetical, numerical, geographic, colour coded, or by date. Alphabetic is the most popular. Label by starting with the broadest category first, the reverse of how we address

an envelope, and keep breaking down to smaller headings, e.g., Properties, Maintenance, Contractors.

3. If the person receiving the mail writes the file name on at time of reading, it doesn't have to be read again in order to decide where to file it.

4. If more than one person is using the system, a cross-reference list may help. Don't go overboard on this, though. Keep it brief. You're not trying to catalogue a library here. If you're using a numerical system, you will also need an index posted in some obvious place.

5. Don't use paper-clips to clip papers together. Staple.

6. There's nothing worse than a filing cabinet you can't get your hand into. Always have enough space to move the files and take things easily in and out.

7. Try pencilling in a 'throw-by' date when you first receive something. Then you don't have to re-read the whole thing later to see whether it's obsolete.

8. Beware of miscellaneous files. They become fat sticky traps with the slightest encouragement! If you have more than a dozen pieces in a miscellaneous file, something will be waiting for its own category.

9. Use an out card of some kind to show that a file is away being used. What you use depends on the kind of file, but it might be a coloured card which stands out like a sore thumb, and has room to write the name of the current user. This can save a lot of frustration and wasted time for people wandering around looking for vital information which has 'mysteriously' not walked its way back to the cabinet.

Filing archival material

There are organisations dedicated to safely storing your archival material. I strongly recommend investigating them. They handle fire, water, and security risks much better than any non-specialist could ever do; they have amazingly efficient retrieval systems which don't cost you an arm and a leg if you want material back for some reason, and they'll even come in and sort out your mess, catalogue it, and tell you what can be discarded and what needs to be kept. The cost is minimal compared with having to do it yourself.

Throw

What stops you from throwing out your obsolete papers?

Consider how you can reduce the amount of material that lands on your desk. Don't ask for written information that you don't need, just to shut someone up.

What subscriptions can you cancel? One of my favourite stories about material received and not read comes from one of my course participants. He is head of a multinational health company. He was telling the group how he received the monthly magazines from all the other national subsidiaries because they gave him good ideas for his own monthly magazine. Suddenly he stopped, with a look of horror on his face.

'I've just realised something,' he said. 'I can't read all the languages!'

The next week he reported that he'd cleaned out, and cancelled!

Check the forms your company uses. Almost everyone can find ways to improve them. Next time they're due for a reprint, have a company brainstorming session to question and improve. Some of the information once required may no longer be needed. You may be able to reduce both questions and forms. Have a Save a Tree day.

Encourage people to do short memos and reports. Reward clarity. I love Mark Twain's pithy little phrase: 'I'm sorry I had to write you a long letter. I didn't have time for a short one.'

We've all suffered at the hand of those who indulge in gobble-de-gook. Death to jargon! If you want a refresher course on unintelligible garbage, try reading the official reports of many government departments, some material from higher learning institutions, and even the writing of some management 'experts'. The authors of these documents don't seem to realise that they're playing ego-stroking games with themselves. Do they know that the rest of the world has no idea what they're talking about? Is it a form of intellectual snobbery, and if so, who's laughing at whom? It is much harder to write simply and clearly than to use the fashionable language of your industry. Those who use long, flowery phrases in preference to clean, honest language are showing intellectual laziness and sloppy practice. If you've got the courage to do it, send such reports back to their originators and ask for a translation. The reaction could be fun!

Bothered by endless unsolicited faxes? Politely ask the senders to take you off their fax list. If they don't listen, and you've asked them several times, you can lay a complaint with Telecom.

A PLACE FOR EVERYTHING AND EVERYTHING IN ITS PLACE

That old adage again! You bet!

Develop a parking system for everything that comes into your office, or your home. Immediately put each thing in its place; you'll find it much more easily next time you need it. It takes time to develop this habit, but doing so greatly repays the effort. You no longer waste precious time searching for the keys, diary, cheque-book, or anything else. The people who always seem to lose glasses and keys only do so because they haven't got a regular place to put them.

This rule also applies to what you keep on and in your desk. Decide which files you want at fingertip reach and which can go in the storeroom or filing cabinet. What will you put in your bottom dump drawer, what sits on the desk, and what goes in the top drawer? A few minutes spent quietly thinking through the sequence of your normal activities will, I promise you, save you hours per week.

ELECTRONIC SYSTEMS

I haven't spent time discussing electronic transfer and storage of information, because it is a specialist field. If used correctly, there can be a huge saving of stored paper, but many of my very computerised clients tell me that if a company doesn't have good manual systems, and clarity about what needs storing, electronic systems will end up being a repository for rubbish just as much as an over-flowing and unpruned old-fashioned filing cabinet. So my recommendation is — know clearly what you need and then talk to the people using electronic systems. Ask around. Find the people who are happy with the systems they use. Don't just rely on the experts. If you can't understand what so-called experts are telling you, go and do some more homework until you do. You could waste a huge amount of time and money setting up systems which don't do what you want.

FINAL POINTERS ON STAYING FABULOUS

Remember — we're all human. Don't beat yourself up if sometimes you slip back into old habits — they take time to change. No matter how perfectly you set up this system there will still be times when you feel as if the dump-truck has called by! I do promise you, however, that if you practise, you will eventually gain an awesome amount of power over your daily work, and you'll use your time so much more effectively. Until I learnt the techniques I've described, I used to be a great little collector, and my desk was regularly messy. The main reason was the lack of a system. Once I learnt to keep materials off my desk unless I was working on them, and became confident that they wouldn't disappear into a black hole, it was six months before my drawers needed a sort-out again. Since then, a tidy desk has just become a habit, like brushing my teeth. It feels uncomfortable when it's not done.

FINAL TIPS
1. Develop a *do it now* mentality.
2. Always ask yourself — does this item have enough value to warrant the time, money, and energy required to save it?
3. Imagine you have an invisible silver cord connecting you to every possession. Does it energise you or emotionally drain you?

Conclusion

I wish you well, as I wave you goodbye

So you want the bottom line on taking control of your life? You see people around you making great strides forward, but so far success seems to be just beyond your grasp? Are you doing the right things to reach your goals, you ask yourself? Is there anything else you need to know? You've been studying about how to use your time better, you've got the theory base, you've got the practical specifics, so how can you capitalise on your new knowledge and make sure you get where you want to go?

You've got it in your grasp. There is no mystique about it — success comes one small step at a time. Every person who achieves their goals in life is very focused on the way they use their time. They have a strong sense that their time is as precious to them as their life blood. Would you waste your blood? Of course not. Don't squander your time either.

What is success to you? What gives you greatest personal satisfaction? Are you prepared to commit to building improved habits. Have you developed the long view? Every extraordinary achievement in human life is the result of thousands of ordinary efforts that are seldom seen or appreciated.

DISCIPLINE

All through this book we've talked about developing self-discipline to prioritise our daily activities. Not a rigid, life-quenching discipline, however, but a method that allows us freedom and flexibility.

By daily doing the most vital and important activities, and including Proactive activities as often as possible, you will enable yourself to reach your goals, whatever they may be. Become result-oriented, not action-oriented. Recognise that this means focusing as much of your action as you can on the long-term. Don't let your days be gobbled up with undirected action, or low-value action — make sure your actions have a focus and purpose.

And, at the same time, keep some balance in your life. Don't ignore your family, friends, and health in a mad scramble towards your goals, or you may be very lonely, sick and tired when you've achieved them.

Be courageous. Take risks. Step out into the unknown. People who play safe and never test their boundaries remain comfortably in their ruts. What is the difference between a rut and a grave? With a rut you have a choice to step out; with a grave you don't!

Don't accept other people's judgment of you. Believe in yourself, and don't focus on your present circumstances. Even when you're not sure where you're going and the path is not clear, keep believing in yourself and your ability to get yourself out of the mud. Not many years ago I was a solo mother with five children and an intellectually handicapped foster son, reliant on a government benefit. I could not get well-paid work in the country town I lived near — government subsidised work schemes were all I could find. The local community leaders didn't want me as their town librarian when the opportunity came up, even though I was the only qualified librarian who applied. The reason that filtered back through the grapevine was that I was a solo mother who might be unreliable! Their small-town thinking did me a favour. Instead of wishing life had dealt me a different hand, or wasting energy arguing the decision with people who didn't want me, I looked for other avenues.

I eventually moved to a big city where I knew virtually nobody. With no friends in high places, no money, no influential family, but a huge amount of determination, self-discipline, willingness to work hard, and an openness to life's possibilities and leadings, I have turned my life around 180 degrees (and that's another story). It wasn't overnight success. In fact, many times it didn't look like success at all. But persistence and belief in myself paid off. I tell you this not to boast or enlist sympathy, but only to encourage. I have lived the principles and techniques I talk about in this book and, dear reader, they work. They are road-tested, and will put you on the highway to whatever success you choose, if you're prepared to do the small unsung steps, day after day.

People who develop a long view and make decisions accordingly are the achievers of life — they will be successful. They know that success is a grand mountain of minute small steps and small decisions. Success comes in the moments when no-one else is looking. It is the accumulation of a lifetime of little actions.

If you doubt me, do your own survey of people whom you consider to be successful. Whatever their chosen path in life, they will have all sacrificed something to reach their present position. We earn what we deserve. I know it's a cliché, but there are no free lunches in life. Nor do well-integrated families and loving relationships happen by themselves. Good fortune is earned, not given!

I'd like to leave you with the words of a few of my favourite authors.

• From Napoleon Hill: 'There are no limitations to the mind, except those we acknowledge.'

- From Anita Roddick, of Body Shop fame: 'I think the older you get the more you realise that this is no dress rehearsal, so you feel you want to put more into life. I am always astonished and grateful, when I wake up in the morning, to be alive. The thought that every day might be my last, and the desire to make the most of every moment, drives me on.'
- And finally from George Bernard Shaw: 'This is the true joy in life . . . being used for a purpose recognised by yourself as a mighty one . . . being a force of Nature instead of a feverish selfish little clod of ailments and grievances complaining that the world will not devote itself to making you happy . . . I am of the opinion that my life belongs to the whole community and as long as I live it is my privilege to do for it whatever I can.

  'I want to be thoroughly used up when I die. For the harder I work the more I live. I rejoice in life for its own sake. Life is no brief candle to me. It's a sort of splendid torch which I've got to hold up for the moment and I want to make it burn as brightly as possible before handing it on to future generations.'

Success is not an accident — it is a decision. Make it happen, and have a great life.

Bibliography and further reading

Allen, Jane Elizabeth. *Beyond Time Management: Organising The Organization*. Addison-Wesley, 1986.

Bach, Richard. *Illusions: The Adventures of a Reluctant Messiah*. Pan Books, 1973.

Blanchard, Kenneth, Oncken, William, Jr., and Burrows, Hal. *The One Minute Manager Meets the Monkey*. Fontana, 1990.

Blanchard, Kenneth, Zigarmi Patricia, and Zigarmi, Drea. *Leadership and the One Minute Manager*. Fontana, 1987.

Bland, Glenn. *Success! the Glenn Bland Method*. Tyndale House, 1972.

Bozek, Phillip E. *50 One-minute Tips to Better Communication: A Wealth of Business Communication Ideas*. Crisp, 1991.

Buzan, Tony, with Buzan, Barry. *The Mind Map Book*. BBC Books, 1993.

Canfield, Jack, and Hansen, Mark Victor. *Chicken Soup for the Soul*. Health Communications, 1993.

Carnegie, Dale. *How to Win Friends and Influence People*. Angus & Robertson, [1936] 1984.

Carroll, Lewis. *The Complete Works of Lewis Carroll*. Random, 1959.

Covey, Stephen R. *7 Habits of Highly Effective People*. Simon & Schuster, 1990.

Covey, Stephen R. and Merrill, A. Roger. *First Things First*. Simon & Schuster, 1994.

de Bono, Edward. *Six Thinking Hats for Schools. Book 4. Resource Book*. Hawker Brownlow Education, 1992.

Dossey, Larry. *Space, Time and Medicine*. New Science Library, 1984.

Douglass, Merrill E. and Douglass, Donna N. *Manage Your Time, Manage Your Work, Manage Yourself*. AMACOM, 1980.

Drucker, Peter F. *The Effective Executive*. Harper & Row, 1966.

Frankl, Viktor E. *Man's Search for Meaning*. Simon & Schuster, [1959] 1984.

Franklin, Benjamin. *The Autobiography of Benjamin Franklin*. A restoration of a fair copy by Max Farrand, University of California, 1949.

Gawain, Shakti. *Creative Visualization*. Bantam, 1979.

Gerber, Michael E. *The E Myth: Why Most Small Businesses Don't Work and What To Do About It*. HarperCollins, 1986.

Giblin, Les. *How to Have Confidence and Power in Dealing with People*. Prentice-Hall, [1956] 1986.

Good News Bible. Collins, 1976.

Halliday, Garry, with Kalaf, Terry and Kingsley, and Disspain, Chris. *Creating Your Fuller LiFE MAP*. Life Maps Global, 1995.

Henderson, Robyn. *Networking for $uccess*. R. Henderson, 1992.

Hill, Napoleon. *Law of Success*. Success Unlimited, 1979.

Hill, Napoleon. *Think and Grow Rich*. Wilshire, [1937] 1966.

Hill, Napoleon. *The Master-Key to Riches*. Ballantine Books, [1965] 1982.

Hodge, Ken. *Sport Motivation: Training Your Mind for Peak Performance*. Reed, 1994.

Hunt, Des. *What Makes People Tick: How to Understand Yourself and Others*. McGraw-Hill, 1991.

Kehoe, John. *Mind Power*. Zoetic, 1987.

Mackenzie, Alec. *The Time Trap*. Business Library, 1990.

Mandino, Og. *The Choice*. Bantam, 1984.

McGee-Cooper, Ann, and Trammell, Duane. *Time Management for Unmanageable People*. Bantam, 1994.

Moir, Anne and Jessel, David. *Brainsex*. Michael Joseph, 1989.

Oncken, William, Jr. *Managing Management Time; Who's Got the Monkey?* Prentice-Hall, 1984.

Pease, Alan. *How to Make Appointments By Telephone.* (Audio). 1992.

Pollar, Odette. *Organizing Your Workspace.* Crisp, 1992.

Price, Carol. *How to Present a Professional Image.* (Audio)

Roddick, Anita. *Body & Soul.* Ebury Press, 1991.

Semler, Ricardo. *Maverick!* Century, 1993.

Sinetar, Marsha. *Do What You Love, The Money Will Follow.* Dell, 1987.

Tracy, Brian. *Time Management for Results.* Brian Tracy, 1991.

Tracy, Brian. *Maximum Achievement: The Proven System of Strategies and Skills That Will Unlock Your Hidden Powers To Succeed.* Simon & Schuster, 1993.

Tracy, Brian. *Personal and Professional Development Strategies.* Seminar notes, 1995.

Treacy, Declan. *Clear Your Desk!* Random Century, 1991.

Turla, Peter, and Hawkins, Kathleen L. *Time Management Made Easy.* Collins, 1990.

Twain, Mark. *Tom Sawyer.* Dent, 1955.

Wilde, Stuart. *Life Was Never Meant To Be a Struggle.* White Dove International, 1987.

Winston, Stephanie. *Getting Organized: The Easy Way to Put Your Life in Order.* Warner, 1991.

Appendix

We trust you have enjoyed reading *Getting a grip on time* and we'd like to send you a bonus.

Just photocopy the order form on the following page and post, fax, or e-mail to Robyn's office to receive a FREE audio-cassette, valued at A$35, of the speech '7 steps to goal-setting success' by Robyn Pearce and Garry Halliday, one of the authors of the LiFE MAP.

If you have ideas to share, questions to ask, or would like to use Robyn's services as a speaker or trainer for your organisation, or as a contributor to your journal, please contact her office at the following address:

Robyn Pearce Time Management
Suite 356/656 Military Road
Mosman, Sydney, NSW 2088, Australia
Tel. 61-2-9904 9182; fax 61-2-9904 9181
E-mail: robynp@time-specialist.com

Order form

Please send me my FREE copy of Robyn and Garry's tape
'7 steps to goal-setting success', valued at A$35.
Post and packaging of A$10 enclosed.

Name: _____

Address: _____

_____

Company: _____

Tel: _____ Fax: _____

E-mail: _____

Mobile: _____

Please make cheques for post and packaging of A$10 payable to
Robyn Pearce Time Management.

☐ Visa   ☐ Bankcard   ☐ Mastercard

☐ American Express   ☐ Diners Card

Credit card no.: _____

Exp. date: _____ Name on card: _____

Signature: _____

Security no. (for Amex only): _____

☐ I wish to know more about your other services, courses,
    speeches, and forthcoming books. Please add me to your
    mailing list.